FRANCESCO VALCANOVER

THE GALLERIES OF THE ACCADEMIA

152 COLOUR PLATES

Room 1
14th. and early 15th. century

Room 2
of the S. Giobbe Altar-piece
by Giovanni Bellini

Room 4
of Andrea Mantegna
and Piero della Francesca

Room 5
of Giovanni Bellini
and Giorgione

Rooms 6, 7 and 8
of the early sixteenth century

Rooms 10 and 11 (first part)
of Titian, Tintoretto
and Paolo Veronese

Room 11 (second part)
Tiepolo

Room 12
18th. century landscape painting

Room 13
Jacopo Bassano

Room 14
of the seventeenth century

Rooms 15, 16, 16a and 17
of the eighteenth century

Room 20
of the stories of the Cross

Room 21
of the Story of St. Ursula

Room 23
of Church of Santa Maria
della Carità

Room 24
of the «Albergo della Scuola»

11
10
9
6
8
7
12
13
5
3
2
4
14
20
21
1
16
16a
15
17
19
18
22
24
23

Printed: January 1995

THE ACCADEMIA GALLERIES

The Academy of painting and sculpture was established in Venice in 1750 under the direction of Giambattista Piazzetta and was accorded official recognition in 1756 when Giambattista Tiepolo became its President. After the fall of the Republic of Venice in 1779 and the annexation of the city to the Italic Kingdom in 1805 the Academy premises were moved from the Fonteghetto della Farina at S. Marco (the building which now houses the Port of Venice Authority) to the buildings previously used as the Church and Scuola della Carità and the Convento dei Canonici Lateranensi which was designed by Andrea Palladio in 1561. The statute of the Academy required that apart from the school there should be a «sala per le statue» where the plaster figures of the Farsetti collection could be housed and a gallery where paintings by the academicians themselves could be hung. The collection of the gallery was considerably enlarged when the Academy acquired many paintings from churches and convents which had been suppressed, including many which Napoleon had taken to Paris. Further additions came in 1816 with the acquisition of the Molin collection, and in 1838 and 1850 when the Contarini and Renier collections were incorporated. Many paintings of the Manfrin collection, including the Mantegna «St. George», were added in 1856. As the Academy galleries acquired new paintings so it needed more space in which to store and display them. In part this was achieved by adapting existing space and in part by constructing new buildings. The church had already been divided into two floors in 1811 and between 1821 and 1834 the two great rooms on the southern side were built and the gallery of Palladio was modified. By 1841 the rooms to the right of the neo-classical entrance hall were completed and by 1856 the old buildings were linked to the new with the completion of the rooms known as the «nuovissime». After the annexation of Venice to the Kingdom of Italy in 1866 and the separation of the Galleries from the school in 1882 the collection of the Galleries underwent its first systematic ordering under the direction of Giulio Cantalamessa (1894-1904) who also initiated a policy of acquisitions, continued by his successor Gino Fogolari (1906-1941). Among the paintings acquired in this period were the «Madonna of the Zodiac» by Cosmè Tura (1896), «St. Jerome» by Jacopo Bassano (1900), the «Pietà» by Giovanni Bellini (1934), «Portrait of a Gentleman» by Lorenzo Lotto (1930), Giambattista Tiepolo's cartoons for the now destroyed ceiling of the Church of the Scalzi (1930) and the «Tempest» by Giorgione (1932). After the Second World War the collection was subjected to a programme of radical examination by Vittorio Moschini (1941-1961) and was re-hung with the invaluable collaboration of Carlo Scarpa. The pictures were cleared of all non-original decorative elements and were displayed in good light, well-spaced and grouped so as to offer the visitor a clear view of the various phases of the development of Venetian art (though even now, the particular arrangement of the rooms and lack of space makes the ideal of a chronologically ordered display unattainable). With the acquisition in recent years of important works by Francesco Maffei, Sebastiano Mazzoni, Giannantonio Pellegrini, Gaspare Traversi, Alessandro Longhi and Francesco Guardi, the Accademia Galleries now offer the most complete and representative collection of five centuries of Venetian art.

ROOM 1

(14th. and early 15th. century)

This huge hall was originally the Chapter House or assembly room of the Gothic Scuola of S. Maria della Carità. A few fragments of the original frescoed frieze have survived as has the carved and gilded wooden ceiling which was probably by Mario Cozzi, famous for his work on the choir at S. Maria dei Frari. The entrance hall and the two flights of stairs date from 1756 when Maccaruzzi completed the remodelling of the facade to the designs of

PAOLO VENEZIANO (working 1333 – died between 1358 and 1362), *Madonna and Child with two Votaries.* Tempera on panel (1,42×0,90) – c. 1325.

Paolo Veneziano, the first great identifiable artist in the history of Venetian painting, was clearly well-acquainted with Byzantine traditions. Indeed he seemed to need to go back to the anachronistic world of Byzantine art to find a means of expression for the most sincere insights of his poetic vision though he must also have been aware of the great advances being made in western art, particulary by the Tuscan masters Giovanni Pisano and Giotto whose work he would have seen at the Scrovegni Chapel in nearby Padua. The «Madonna and Child with two Votaries», still in its original red and blue notched frame, is a good example of Paolo's personal blending of mainland art with the iconic and aulic idioms of Byzantine tradition. The resulting image is completely oriental in feeling. The Virgin sits rigid on the throne and holds out the Child for the adoration of the devotees. The Child is surrounded by a blue mandorla in accordance with a Syrian iconographic schema. But the liveliness of the drawing of the sacred and human figures in the background makes them stand out from their gold setting in a way which is not entirely untypical of the stiff, wooden figures which populate the work of contemporary painters of religious images working in the Veneto-Byzantine style. Thus the artist brings together western formal components and Byzantine compositional schemes in his personal vision of colour.

Giorgio Massari. The two statues representing Faith and Charity were by Gian Maria Morlaiter and were set in their position on the staircases in 1765. Today the paintings housed in this room follow Venetian art from its beginnings in the work of the first identifiable masters Paolo and Lorenzo who revitalized the Byzantine figurative tradition with their own personal and western accents, through its slow entry into the mainstream of International Gothic art around the end of the 14th. century and during the first half of the 15th. century with the work of Gentile da Fabriano in the Palazzo Ducale between 1409 and 1416 and that of Pisanello after 1419.

PAOLO VENEZIANO, *Polyptych.* Tempera on panel (1,67×2,85 overall) – c. 1350.

The development of the art of Paolo Veneziano is characterized by a kind of see-sawing supremacy of one or the other of two influences: on the one hand, the advances being made in contemporary Italian painting and on the other the traditions of oriental figurative art. In this polyptych, set in the sumptuousness of its magnificent International Gothic wooden frame each of the novelties of western art tends to find its expression within the Byzantine modes typical of Byzantine art at the time of the Palaeologus dynasty. Physical and spiritual centre of the complex iconographical scheme is the «Coronation of the Virgin», surrounded by eight stories from the life of Christ. On the left are «The Adoration of the Magi», «The Baptism of Christ», «The Last Supper» and «The Prayer in the Garden and the Arrest of Christ»; on the right are «The Journey to Calvary», «The Crucifixion», «The Resurrection and the encounter with Mary Magdalene» and «The Ascension». In the second order, set between the four Evangelists, are scenes depicting, from left to right: «Pentecost», «St. Clare taking the Veil», «St. Francis handing back his clothes to his father», «The Stigmata of St. Francis», «The Death of St. Francis» and «Christ in Judgement». The contrast of the Gothic inventiveness of the figures and the planimetric effects of the gilded background of the panels with the «Coronation of the Virgin» is even more noticeable in many of the lesser scenes such as «The Adoration of the Magi» and «The Baptism of Christ» which are clearly reminiscent of Byzantine treatments of the same subjects. The influence of the West on the other hand, is suggested by the lively handling of the compositional rhythms in other stories from the life of Christ such as «The Prayer in the Garden and the Arrest of Christ» and «The Crucifixion».

LORENZO VENEZIANO (known 1356-1372), *The Lion Polyptych.* Tempera on panel (2,58×4,32 overall) – 1357-59.

While the second half of the fourteenth century saw artists like Guariento, Giusto de' Menabuoi, Altichiero and Tommaso da Modena working in Padua and Treviso and bringing Gothic painting to its finest flowering in the Veneto, in Venice itself there were very few who showed any signs of being influenced by the lively scene on the mainland. The greatest of those who did was Lorenzo Veneziano who, like Paolo, overcame the contradictions between the western and eastern worlds by trusting to the ineffable sensuousness of colour, the fundamental and most moving component of Venetian painting. But Lorenzo, much more than Paolo, inclined towards Gothic culture for his means of expression. Clear evidence of this tendency is seen in the great polyptych in the collection of the Gallery. The panels were completed in 1359 for the Venetian church of S. Anthony Abbot, commissioned by Domenico Lion who had held temporary membership of the Venetian Senate in 1356 and 1357. In the «Annunciation» of the central panel traditional iconography is set aside and the airy, three-quarter length figure of the Virgin is moved from the centre to leave more space for the angel in the act of making his annunciation. In the foreshortened image above the Virgin's head the Eternal Father seems almost to be launching the dove forwards. The subtle play of physical poses and spiritual attitudes achieves a life-like quality never before seen in Venice, and in the figures of the saints in the side panels too the rhythms are sinuous and relaxed. The colour, not attempting to obey the coded decorativism of Veneto-Byzantine tradition, takes on a lively timbre and a refined range of shadings: blues, reds and greens paling into pearl-grey and light-pink reflections, fading into pure luminosity. Examples of this formal refinement, where already the fundamental characteristics of Venetian Gothic style are clearly present, can be seen in the half-length figures of Saints in the upper order of the polyptych; a whole range of human types caught in a variety of different poses.

LORENZO VENEZIANO, *Marriage of St. Catherine.* Tempera on panel (0,95×0,58) – 1359.

At times the painting of Lorenzo Veneziano is charged with gentle naturalism, as in this «Marriage of St. Catherine», signed and dated 2nd. February, 1359 (more Veneto). The painting was certainly painted as the central panel of a polyptych. The way the Virgin holds her Son as He almost slips from her knee to place the ring on the finger of St. Catherine is finely observed and rendered, while the angels, all intent on playing their musical instruments, seem to go beyond the limits of the picture itself. The fluid handling of movement is very reminiscent of the impetuous gothicism of Vitale di Bologna, while the soft, gentle range of colours and the careful attention to detail in the figures of St. Catherine and her companion recall the tender realism of Tommaso da Modena.

LORENZO VENEZIANO, *Annunciation.* Tempera on panel (1,11×0,54) – 1371.

This painting, signed and dated 1371, was the central panel of a polyptych and was donated to the Galleries' collection in 1816 by the legate Molin. Here we can see clearly how Lorenzo Veneziano, in his mature work, moved increasingly towards the musical expressiveness of colour shot through with Gothic accents. The iconographical scheme of this «Annunciation» is radically different from that of the Lion polyptych. The figures of the Virgin and the herald angel inhabit the space of the picture in a much more substantial sense, are in much solider bodily contact with the grass and flowers. Indeed this is the first example in Venice of a naturalistic motif which was dear to the hearts of the refined artists working in the International Gothic style. This style too is exemplified in the elaborate linear cadences and the way the figures are presented in curving compositional rhythms.

MCCCLXXV · D MEXE · D
MARÇO · CHATARINUS
· PINXIT

◀ **CATARINO** (known 1362-1382), *Coronation of the Virgin.* Tempera on panel (0,89×0,58) – 1375.

Paolo and Lorenzo Veneziano had no direct followers even though the few painters of some importance in Venice around the end of the fourteenth century went their way without paying too much attention to the stylistic suggestions originating from the nearby mainland, the most important of which were the developments in the International Gothic style, particularly in Verona and Lombardy. Thus Catarino, in his «Coronation of the Virgin» dated 1375, strives after plastic effects of a certain intensity and convincing spacial suggestions without however abandoning the traditional iconographic scheme for the subject nor the supremacy of the ornate play of colour.

JACOBELLO ALBEREGNO (died before 14th. July, 1397), *Triptych.* Tempera on panel (0,45×0,56) – Second half of the XVI century.

Much more of an innovator than either Catarino or Lorenzo Veneziano was Jacobello Alberegno who, in the Galleries' Triptych with Crucifixion and Saints, his only signed work, reveals himself to be an artist of penetrating refinement. If it is true that the two lateral saints, St. Gregory and St. Jerome, are examples of stylized Gothic figures, the images of the small central panel display a naturalness worthy of one of the best of Giotto's disciples. An extraordinary human dimension seems to govern the expression of sentiments in the picture: a grief-stricken St. John the Evangelist clutches his cloak to his breast while the Virgin extends imploring arms and stares transfixed with anguish at her crucified Son.

◀ **JACOBELLO ALBEREGNO,** *Vision of St. John the Evangelist.* Tempera on panel (0,95×0,61) – Second half of the XIVth. century.

The ineffably expressive naturalness which makes the central panel of the signed triptych so admirable appears again in the panels of the Polyptych with five episodes from the Apocalypse, originally placed in the church of St. John the Evangelist at Torcello. In the central panel for example, where St. John the Evangelist looks up from his writing to admire the Eternal in glory with the Lamb of God, surrounded by the symbols of the four Evangelists with wings covered with eyes, being worshipped by twenty-four venerable old men, here too the theme, though very complex, comes through with exemplary clarity because of the subtle expressiveness of the details which frees the sacred vision of every transcendent abstraction.

JACOBELLO ALBEREGNO, *The Harvest of the World.* Tempera on panel (0,45×0,33) – Second half of the XIVth. century.

Even more in the four minor panels of the Polyptych of the Apocalypse the transcendental significance of the gold background pales before the freshness and inventiveness of Jacobello Alberegno's imagination. As with the other scenes, so with the «Harvest of the World», the text of the Book of the Apocalypse (XIII, vv. 17-18) is closely followed: «And another angel came out of the temple... and he too had a sharpened sickle. And another angel came out from the altar... saying: wield your sharpened sickle and harvest the grapes of the world, for the fruit is now ripe». The detailed and penetrating transcription of the sacred text into pictorial form seems to be softened by the enchanting addition of an arbour of black grapes with bunches of the fruit hanging heavy with juice and leaves which are already showing signs that Autumn is drawing to a close.

NICOLÒ DI PIETRO (known 1394-1430), *Madonna and Child and a Devotee.* Tempera on panel (1,07×0,65) – 1394.

While the chief influence on Alberegno was his experience of the artists working in Padua, Giusto de' Menabuoi in particular, Nicolò di Pietro absorbed influences from even further afield, from Emilia to the Rhineland and Bohemia. The result of this tendency to be interested in what was happening in other cultural centres was that Nicolò di Pietro from 1494 (the date on the «Madonna and Child and a Devotee») became the most important Venetian artist working during the period of transition to International Gothic style. In this panel the traditional iconography is respected, even to the miniscule proportions of the figure of Vulciano Belgarzone da Zara who commissioned the painting, kneeling at the feet of the Virgin. But the decorative abstraction of Paolo Veneziano no less than the refined elegance of Lorenzo Veneziano have now gone for ever and in their place is a confident human sense which pervades every figure represented plastically within a composition conceived with precise intentions of rendering a definite spacial entity.

JACOBELLO DEL FIORE, *Justice between the Archangels Michael and Gabriel.* Tempera on panel ▶ (2,08×4,90) – 1421.

In his early work, Jacobello del Fiore was clearly working within the modes of Venetian painting of the late fourteenth century. But as soon as he came into contact with Gentile da Fabriano whom the Republic of Venice had summoned in 1414-1415 to decorate the Great Council Chamber of the Palace of the Doges with his International Gothic «fables», he tended to shake free of all the abstract precepts of Byzantine art and develop a narrative fluency and a stylization of shapes and forms which reflected the spirit of «courtly» Gothic style. He adopted this style when dealing with official themes too, as in the «Triptych of Justice» painted in 1421 for the offices of the Magistrato del Proprio at the Palace of the Doges.

JACOBELLO DEL FIORE (known 1394-1439), *Triptych of the Madonna della Misericordia*. Tempera on panel (0,86×1,13) – c. 1415.

The Triptych was painted between 1415 and 1436 with the earlier of the two dates the more probable given the affinity of this work with the style of the «Stories of Santa Lucia» in the Pinacoteca at Fermo. If the appearance of the lateral saints – St. John the Baptist and St. John the Evangelist – is still somewhat forbidding, and if they seem still to be firmly part of the world of the 1300s, the centre is occupied by the Virgin presented as an extremely elegant, divine idol, surrounded by crowds of devotees, the costume and physical attitude of each of which is rendered through an extremely subtle use of light and colour.

JACOBELLO DEL FIORE, *Coronation of the Virgin.* Tempera on panel (2,83×3,03) – c. 1438.

The rich, exuberant decorativism of the «Triptych of Justice» is the final moment of involution in the art of Jacobello del Fiore who, in his final phase, seemed almost to engage in a mental journey back in time and style towards the archaic. Thus his model for the «Coronation of the Virgin», finished in 1438 for the High Altar of the Cathedral at Ceneda, was Guariento's great fresco of the same subject, painted between 1366 and 1368 for the Great Council Chamber of the Palace of the Doges. But the powerful architectural clarity of the fourteenth century model is diminished in Jacobello's version and becomes a stylized repetition of figurative motifs, almost swarming around the insistent centre-piece of the Coronation of the Virgin. At the foot of the throne which seems to unfold from the ground like an extraordinary marble flower, kneels the proud figure of Bishop Antonio Correr who commissioned the painting.

MICHELE GIAMBONO (known 1420-1462), *Coronation of the Virgin.* Tempera on panel (2,29×1,76) – c. 1448.

After a probable initiation at the workshop of Jacobello del Fiore, followed by a phase of admiration of Gentile da Fabriano, Michele Giambono soon passed to a sweetened form of Gothicism with somewhat affected colourings rather along the lines of Pisanello's work in the Palace of the Doges in Venice. The «Coronation of the Virgin» which in fact has a clearly Gothic air about it, can probably be identified as the panel commissioned from Giambono in 1447 by Giovanni Dotto for the Church of St. Agnese. Attached to the order were the conditions that it should be delivered by the end of 1448 and that it should be similar to the one, painted not many years before by Antonio Vivarini and Giovanni d'Alemagna for the Venetian church of S. Pantalon.

MICHELE GIAMBONO, *Polyptych of St. James.* Tempera on panel (central panel 1,09×0,44; side panels 0,88×0,29 each) – c. 1450.

Originally from the Scuola del Cristo at the Giudecca, the polyptych is composed of five panels, the central one of which is of St. James the Greater with St. John the Evangelist and the Venerable Felice Pelizzi, the founder of the Order of Servites on the left, and St. Michael the Archangel and St. Louis of Toulouse on the right. The figures of the saints are set in a slow, semicircular rhythm against the tooled gold of the background and the actual paint seems to be translucent like porcelain. The extremely refined figures suggest obvious affinities with the world of Pisanello, particularly the figure of the Archangel Michael in his heavy armour decorated with gold, his pale face encircled with a crown of curls, his body poised almost as if to execute a dance-step over that of the dragon which lies like a heraldic image at the bottom of the panel. Again in this late work, Giambono's confidence in his world of fabled lands and airy architecture, of gently flowing arabesques and elegantly shaded colourings will certainly not have been shaken by the presence in Venice since 1442 of an example of the new art emerging from Tuscany the frescoes of Andrea del Castagno in the chapel of St. Tarasius in the Church of San Zaccaria.

ANTONIO VIVARINI (1415 c. – 1476/84), *Virgin and Child*. Tempera on panel (0,56×0,41) – c. 1440.

While at Padua and even in Venice itself some of the main figures of the new art of Tuscany were working to the laws of perspective and in the conviction of the conscious dignity of man as an individual, Venetian painting reacted to the promptings of the new culture almost with reluctance, filtering them through a vision which in substance was still Gothic. This is the context of the work of Antonio Vivarini and Jacopo Bellini (cfr. p. 26), both founders of dynasties of artists, and both crucial figures in the period of transition in Venice from the first to the second half of the fifteenth century. This «Madonna and Child» belongs to Antonio Vivarini's earliest period and is characterized by a certain plasticity of shape and form arising out of the gentle throbbing of the chiaroscuro and the luminous timbre of the colour.

ANTONIO VIVARINI, *Marriage of St. Monica*. Tempera on panel (0,46×0,31) – 1441.

This small panel, together with others which have recently been identified, made up an altar-piece dedicated to St. Monica in the Church of S. Stefano in Venice. The domestic scene is set in the courtyard of a bourgeois household and embodies Antonio Vivarini's timid attempts at rendering spacial perspective. It demonstrates too the extent to which his world, suspended between the new and the old, acknowledged the importance of Renaissance rules. In contrast with the uncertain definition of the architecture in terms of perspective, the details of costume and the physical and spiritual gestures of the characters are carefully recorded.

ROOM 2

(of the S. Giobbe Altar-piece by Giovanni Bellini)

Constructed in 1875 to provide a worthy setting for the Titian «Assumption» which had come into the Galleries' collection in the early nineteenth century as a result of the suppression of the churches and convents during the Napoleonic era. The «Assumption» itself was returned to the Church of S. Maria dei Frari in 1919 but the magnificent room still contains several memorable examples of the altar-piece, which was the form of artistic expression most typical of Venetian religious painting in the second half of the fifteenth century. The composition of the altar-piece sets the sacred figures in a precise architectural context ranging them in direct frontal view on planes which relate to the plane of the frame in terms of the most rigorous perspective. The world thus conceived has a motionless quality, a majestic harmony described in the limpid, transparent air of the clearest hour of the day and one feels the confidence with which the humanistic veneration of beauty is expressed, the classical nobility with which it is experienced and evoked.

GIOVANNI BELLINI (1430 c.-1516), *The S. Giobbe Altarpiece.* Tempera on panel (4,71×2,58) – c. 1487.

This magnificent altar-piece, painted for the second altar on the right in the Church of S. Giobbe, is one of the most important of all Giovanni Bellini's (cfr. pp. 28-37) considerable output. Its monumental conception is still reminiscent of the masterpiece painted in 1476 by Antonello da Messina for the Church of S. Cassiano (cfr. p. 122) though the hint at perfect geometrical shapes and crystal-clear colours in this latter piece becomes little more than a common softness of communicative style in the Bellini painting. A warm light, reflected and diffused by the gold of the mosaic, bathes the Virgin and saints who, in groups of three – Francis, John the Baptist and Job on the left and Dominic, Sebastian and Louis on the right – stand at the sides in a converging human scene which contains too the three beautiful angels with their musical instruments ranged on the steps of the throne. The image which emerges is one of profound interior classicism, completely lacking any programmatic imposition in its natural felicity where the human and the divine live together in a serene, comforting and exquisitely poetic conception of the world.

GIAMBATTISTA CIMA DA CONEGLIANO (1459 c. – 1517/18), *Madonna of the Orange Tree.* Tempera and oil on panel (2,12×1,39) – c. 1495.

The greatest of the admirers of Antonello da Messina was Giambattista Cima da Conegliano who maintained the poetic purity of his predecessor's language which was characterized by groups of figures restfully disposed, by the purity of his line, by the airy clarity of his light and by the Spring-like freshness of his colour. Amongst the very finest works in all

Cima's serenely poetic output was the «Madonna of the Orange Tree», originally placed in the Church of Santa Chiara on Murano. With trusting simplicity, the Virgin, seated on an outcrop of rock before the beautiful orange tree, offers the Child to the adoration of St. Louis of France and St. Jerome whilst in the background St. Joseph looks after the ass which has carried the Holy Family to this secluded spot which bears all the signs of having been based on the gently rolling foothills of the Alps in the Veneto. Through the transfiguring strength of the light, which is as if filtered through the clearest of crystal, the idyllic serenity of the countryside and of the sentiments achieves a supreme integrity of expression.

GIAMBATTISTA CIMA DA CONEGLIANO, *The Incredulity of St. Thomas with St. Magno Vescovo.* Tempera and oil on panel (2,15×1,51) – c. 1505.

Even after Giorgione (cfr. p. 38) had introduced his revolutionary «tonal» reform, Giambattista Cima continued with his own lines of expression – his figures statue-like in their firmness and his colours richly limpid. These are the qualities we find in works of his that date from the first decade of the sixteenth century, works like «The Incredulity of St. Thomas and St. Magno Vescovo» for example, which was painted for the Guild headquarters of the Stone-masons at S. Samuele. Spaced with perfect harmony amid the sharp interplay of light and shade, the figures of Christ, of the Apostle and the saint stand statue-like and monumental against the perfectly matching marble slabs of a niche which seems to have been conjured into existence in the dreamy beauty of the countryside of the Veneto. Human figures, architecture and countryside all partake of the same sublime, formal heightening, images of an uncorrupted and incorruptible world, of a timeless, mythically serene present.

VITTORE CARPACCIO (1465 c. – 1523/26), *Presentation of Jesus in the Temple.* Tempera on panel (4,21×2,36) – 1510.

In preparing the altar-piece to decorate the third altar on the right in the Church of S. Giobbe, Venice, Vittore Carpaccio certainly kept in mind the magnificent panel painted by Giovanni Bellini for the same church little more than twenty years before. Compared with Bellini's picture, the marble sections of Carpaccio's niche are even more monumental and the figures more nicely balanced in their perfectly judged movements, including those of the angels intent on playing their instruments, the crumhorn, the lute and the lyre. And each passage of the perfect formal structure is lent firm definition by the light which slants in from the right and strikes cold gleams from the incorruptible pictorial subject. Once again, Carpaccio offers an expression of his humanistic vision through which he measures the visible world on a limpid, reflecting grid of space, colour, light and shade.

MARCO BASAITI (known 1496-1530), *Christ Praying in the Garden.* Oil on panel (3,71×2,24) – 1516. ➧

Marco Basaiti, an admirer of Antonello da Messina and Giovanni Bellini found himself fascinated at the beginning of the sixteenth century by the new artistic manner pioneered by Giorgione (cfr. p. 38). Already in «Christ Praying in the Garden» which adorned the first altar on the right in the Church of S. Giobbe and which belonged to the family of Francesco Foscari, the influence of the style of Antonello (visible in the integrity of colour of the figures and the arrangement of saints at the sides of the portico, of the apostles, and of Christ absorbed in prayer) gives way in the landscape to lyrically dreaming passages clearly drawing their spirit from Giorgione. Though this panel may not exactly offer a complete synthesis of the late fifteenth century world with the dazzling innovations of the early years of the sixteenth century, it is nevertheless emblematic of the meeting-point of two of the finest ages of Venetian painting.

ROOM 4 (of Andrea Mantegna and Piero della Francesca)

Around the middle of the fifteenth century, stimulated by the example of many Tuscan artists, Donatello in particular, Andrea Mantegna began to develop his nostalgic «archeological» version of the new Tuscan ethical norm, founded on the consideration of man as the focal point of all sense-reality. Even before the humanistic fervour of Andrea Mantegna aroused new ferment in the Veneto and Northern Italy in general, Piero della Francesca had already written his admirable «Synthesis of the perspective of form and colour» (Longhi). The proud theories of Andrea Mantegna, no less than the supreme equivalence of form and colour propounded by Piero della Francesca, exerted a profound influence on Giovanni Bellini who, in contrast with his father Jacopo and other contemporary artists like the Vivarinis, Cosme' Tura and Carlo Crivelli, finally broke completely with the mediaeval world, confidently took his place in the civilization of the Renaissance and in fact became one of the new age's finest artists.

PIERO DELLA FRANCESCA (1410/20-1492), *St Jerome and a Devotee*. Tempera on panel (0,49×0,42) – c. 1450.

In his formative years as a painter Piero della Francesca was exposed to the influence of the most important aspects of Florentine art: Maso's bold use of large areas of colour, the perspective-spacial synthesis of Masaccio, the fresh palette of Masolino, the magically organized space of Paolo Uccello and the brightly lit expanses of Domenico Veneziano. From this emerges a highly abstract language where the appearance of what is visible for the first time inhabits a space which is its own measure, without mysteries, without anguish, where form and colour are given equal value, where the visible subject is rendered in an impassive and supremely natural «stasis». The «St. Jerome» picture dates from Piero della Francesca's youth and was perhaps painted in Venice. In the crystal-clear prism of space created by the motionless landscape, the saint and the devotee freely take their place, geometrical shapes no less rigorous than the two tree trunks: the one on the left in the shape of a short cylinder with the Crucifix in the centre, the other on the right, laden with leafy fronds etched against the bright sky. Every detail of the composition submits to the firm control of the perspective and solemnly takes its precisely assigned place in the scheme of related colours and shapes.

ANDREA MANTEGNA (1431-1506), *St. George.* Tempera on panel (0,66×0,32) – c. 1460.

In Padua there were many admirers of Donatello and the other Tuscan artists, but it was Andrea Mantegna who, with his frescoes in the Ovetari Chapel of the Church of the Eremitani, executed when he was just twenty years old, emerged as the reference point for the rebirth of painting over much of Northern Italy and Central Europe. In a romantic dream of the rediscovery of a classical measure, the world of Andrea Mantegna assumes a form in almost metaphysical terms where images stand out with solid plasticity in a space which has been rigorously marked out according to the extremely precise rules of perspective. This severe formal abstraction softens a little as far as the colour is concerned after Mantegna's visit to Venice to meet the Bellinis, whose sister Nicolosia the artist had married. The «St. George» of the Accademia Galleries dates from a period later than the visit to Venice but before Andrea Mantegna left Padua forever in 1460 for the court of the Marquis Ludovico Gonzaga at Mantova. The saint stands serenely impassive in the marble enclosed space, just enough to one side to allow a bird's-eye view of the walled city from which leads the road he has just travelled to engage in his battle with the dragon. Against the stony landscape over which the cloud-laden sky hangs impassively, the figure of the saint within an incisively drawn outline is rendered with perfect perspective in the steady glare of light. Every detail seems to be inlaid in semi-precious stones; the metallic halo, the pure face, the elegant tournament armour, the open hand on his left side. This insistent interpretation leads to a definite and heroic monumental quality in the figure of the saint who is offered not as a symbol of Christian piety but rather of a new, much-yearned-for antiquity.

COSMÈ TURA (1430 c.-1495), *The Madonna of the Zodiac.* Tempera on panel (1,21×0,69) – c. 1453.

Among the many young artists working in Padua who were excited by Donatello's bronzes in the Basilica del Santo, Cosme' Tura, a native of Ferrara, was outstanding for the very special interpretation he offered of Renaissance naturalism. In works like the youthful «Madonna of the Zodiac» which is still in its original magnificent frame and which bears the sign of St. Bernardino at the top between two angels, it is clear how Tura tries to reconcile the distracting refinements of Gothic style with the rational qualities of the new artistic language introduced at the beginning of the century by the Tuscans. The Virgin and Child within the firm grid of perspective seem to be embossed in full relief inside the insurmountable surrounding line. And it is with the attention of the naturalistic Gothic artist that Tura paints the beautiful bunches of black grapes held by two gold-finches at the side of the Virgin. The image contains a preview of the direction Tura's art was to take, with its fierce plasticity and almost obsessively dramatic tension.

HANS MEMLING (1433 c. – 1494), *Portrait of a Young Man.* Oil on panel (0,26×0,20) – before c. 1473.

The vision of man and the world free from the transcendental conception of the Middle Ages achieved on the threshold of the fifteenth century in Tuscany through the laws of linear perspective, was reached almost at the same time in Flanders in an empirical fashion through the continuous lyrical modulation of light which, embracing form and space in a unified synthesis, brings out the natural value and weight of colours. This is the background to the intimate, contemplative, natural quality of the painting of Hans Memling, an excellent example of which is the «Portrait of a Young Man». The light gently explores the features of the human face and of landscape and evokes each detail with incomparable naturalness. The consonance of the spiritual attitude in the figure and nature as expressed by Memling through light and colour certainly did not fail to fascinate the artists of Venice.

JACOPO BELLINI (known from 1424 to 1470), *Madonna and Child Blessing.* Tempera on panel (0,94×0,66) – c. 1455.

Jacopo Bellini, who had perhaps worked as an assistant to Gentile da Fabriano in Florence in 1423, interpreted the laws of linear perspective and plastic form adopted by the Tuscan artists working in Padua in a spirit which was in effect still Gothic. He had frequent contact with the Tuscan artists working in Padua, where in fact in 1453 his daughter Nicolosia married Andrea Mantegna, and tended to interpret the laws of linear perspective and plastic form to which they worked in a spirit which was still substantially Gothic. He therefore shows a predilection in his paintings for the musical linear rhythms and the bright range of colours typical of the International Gothic style and at times for a grave Byzantine solemnity though this latter is compositionally more spacious in his version. A typical example of this tendency towards archaicism is the «Madonna and Child Blessing» where an impenetrable ground of small cherubs' heads etched in gold forms the base for the image.

GIOVANNI BELLINI (1430 c. – 1516), *Madonna and Child Blessing.* Tempera on panel (0,79×0,63) – c. 1470.

The picture, was originally hung in the offices of the Magistrato del Monte Nuovissimo at Palazzo dei Camerlenghi in Venice. It still retains clear evidence of contact with the world of Mantegna though the graphic and plastic values which are so boldly expressed inhabit the same space as the dense chromatic texture which is so vibrant and responsive to the several degrees of light on the dark background. The stiff severity of the perspective-drawing lesson of Mantegna has by now relaxed into an expressive liveliness whose foundation is in the new, human relationship of light and colour.

GIOVANNI BELLINI, *Madonna adoring the sleeping Child.* Tempera on panel (1,20×0,63) – c. 1473.

The new relationship of form and colour sealed by the quality of light leads to results of ineffable human participation in the «Madonna and Child Sleeping» which originally hung in the offices of the Magistrato della Milizia del Mare in the Palace of the Doges. The Virgin is seated with charming naturalness on the marble throne which is reminiscent of Donatello, and joins her sensitive hands in a gesture of mute adoration of her Son who lies fully relaxed in sleep across her knees. The chromatic values of the painting are reminiscent of the way Piero della Francesca used colour in the mid-fifteenth century to unfold the perspective of his images.

GIOVANNI BELLINI, *Madonna and Child between St. Catherine and St. Mary Magdalene*. Tempera and oil on panel (0,58×1,07) – c. 1490.

An excellent example of the special skill of Giovanni Bellini in using light effects to detach images from their backgrounds can be seen in his «Madonna and Child between St. Catherine and St. Mary Magdalene» where the sacred figures stand out not against a landscape but rather against a dense blackish backcloth. The forms take shape and substance in the light in a concert of musical gestures and deep, warm colours judged to exactly the right degree of refinement. While the Virgin in the centre of the group seems to be turning slowly, and St. Catherine on the left, her hair fashionably dressed with strings of pearls, lingers ecstatically in mute adoration, Mary Magdalene emerges from the black of the background in a Leonardesque apparition, her fair, silken tresses hanging loose over her shoulders.

ROOM 5 (of Giovanni Bellini and Giorgione)

No less fundamental than the preceding ones, the experience of the calculated formal abstraction of the San Cassiano altar-piece painted in 1476 by Antonello da Messina led Giovanni Bellini towards a spacious, carefully designed monumental quality which is deliberately softened by the perfect balance of the relationship between space and colour. Giovanni Bellini undertook a ceaseless, tireless search throughout the early years of the sixteenth century for a new, original poetic interpretation of reality, a reality in which figure and landscape attain to a wonderfully solemn and moving unity within idealized representations. Following along the road opened up by Giovanni Bellini, Giorgione launched modern painting, re-applying himself with lyrical abandon to colour which, completely independent from linear-perspective laws, softens in tonal shades according to the brightness of the chromatic planes. In the new world, where the human figure loses all its heroic prominence, Giorgione achieves effects of panic and sensual naturalism through which he expresses the lyrically intimate dreams of his humanistic vision, open as it was to Neo-Platonic philosophy and the Arcadian idyll.

GIOVANNI BELLINI, *Madonna and Child Blessing.* Tempera on panel (0,78×0,60) – c. 1475.

Giovanni Bellini's feeling for landscapes continued to deepen throughout his career. In this panel, behind the solemnly arranged figures of the Virgin and the Child in the act of blessing, there opens out a stupendous view of obviously Veneto landscape. The clear atmosphere in which the verdant plain stretches away past the half-lit city dominated by its bell-tower and the castle caught by the rays of the sun up to the foot-hills and the snow-capped mountains also surrounds the translucent freshness of the colour of the two sacred figures.

GIOVANNI BELLINI, *Madonna of the Little Trees.* Tempera and oil panel (0,78×0,58) – c. 1487.

Signed and dated 1487, the «Madonna of the Little Trees» is perhaps the most well-known of all the many versions Bellini produced of the subject which was closest to his heart. The picture gained its name from the two small trees which stand either side of the Madonna and which perhaps symbolize the Old and New Testaments. A feeling of tranquil harmony of forms and colours informs the grouping of the figures: the gaze of the Madonna and the Child downturned in contemplative silence, their hands entwined in a knot of musical elegance. From the ecstatic group, the eye passes easily to the grassy plain which rises gently to the hills in the distance. Matching the sweetly solemn composition of the picture is the delicate harmony of colours which range through infinitely subtle shadings from dark shadows and soft half-lights to the warm brightness of the afternoon sun.

GIOVANNI BELLINI, *Head of the Redeemer.* Oil on panel (0,33×0,22) – c. 1500.

Around the beginning of the sixteenth century the art of Giovanni Bellini achieves a new sensibility distinguished by the gently shaded but intensely luminous modulation of colour. This new, modern style is certainly the context of the «Head of the Redeemer» which is a fragment of an altar-piece depicting the Transfiguration. Another fragment of the same work, also in the Galleries' collection, shows a scroll which bears the writing «JOANNES BELLINUS ME PINXIT». Uniting light and shade, the head of Christ stretches upwards in ecstasy, conscious of His dual nature, human and divine, a symbol of the idealized message of the artist.

◀ **GIOVANNI BELLINI,** *Allegory of Fickle Fortune.* Tempera and oil on panel (0,34×0,22) – c. 1490.

This and three other small panels, all of which entered the Galleries' collection as part of the Contarini donation in 1838 were decorations for a piece of furniture, perhaps the «restelo» (a mirror and shelf on which ladies hung toilet articles) mentioned by the artist Vincenzo Catena in his will on the 15th. April, 1530. The four allegories display clear classicist leanings and a tendency to elegance of drawing. In the «Allegory of Fickle Fortune» (which has also been interpreted as an allegory of Melancholy or of Venus Genetrix), the female figure and the «putti» are painted with the sharp clarity of a cameo against the dark greenish colour of the lightly ruffled surface of the water. The flesh and garments of the figures seem to draw their colour from the light reflected by the great opaline globe. The painting as a whole is characterized by conciseness and purity of line and achieves poetic unity through the finely balanced relationship of space and colour.

GIOVANNI BELLINI, *Allegory of Prudence.* Tempera and oil on panel (0,34×0,22) – c. 1490.

It is possible that this small panel decorated the «restelo» mentioned by Vincenzo Catena, and it has otherwise been interpreted as an Allegory of Vanity and also as an Allegory of Truth. In preparing this panel Giovanni Bellini would almost seem to have had in mind the statue of Eve made for the Palace of the Doges by the great Veronese sculptor Antonio Rizzo who was active in Venice in the second half of the fifteenth century; the Nordic formal stylization of the female nude as she appears as if turning on the pedestal decorated with a skull motif is very reminiscent of the earlier work. The geometric severity of the human figure is found also in the polished arrangement of closely matching marble slabs covering the walls of the room which contains too the three small children so intent on their musical instruments.

GIOVANNI BELLINI, *Pietà*. Oil on panel (0,65×0,87) – c. 1505.

As the first decade of the sixteenth century unfolded Giovanni Bellini saw growing around him the revolutionary artistic style of Giorgione and also the no less innovatory style of his followers, Titian and Sebastiano del Piombo. Stimulated by so many new departures in contemporary painting, the aged Bellini renewed his own style and strove after a complete integration of his human subjects with the landscape around them, as in this «Pietà». The mourning figure of the Mother and her dead Son are set in a landscape which uses real buildings for its models: on the left for example, can be seen the Basilica at Vicenza (as it was, of course, before Palladio's modifications), the Tower of Piazza dei Signori and the Cathedral of Vicenza, the Church of S. Vitale and the round bell-tower of the Church of S. Apollinare Nuovo at Ravenna. But the concrete quality lent by the real setting in fact is overpowered in overall effect by the nobly classical way in which every form is rendered in limpid, memorable, expressive purity so that the result is definitely an idealized presentation.

GIOVANNI BELLINI, *Madonna and Child between St. John the Baptist and a female Saint.* Oil on panel (0,54×0,76) – c. 1505.

Even clearer in this painting than in the «Pietà» is Giovanni Bellini's intention to relate figures to landscape in an ineffable harmony of light, form and colour. The line still delimits the vivid patches of colour of which the picture is composed. The sacred figures are disposed within spacious triangles, each absorbed in his own thoughts, and the colours of their garments, reds, yellow oranges, greens and blues, blend brilliantly into the stupendous landscape. The view is dominated on the left by a castle which is reminiscent of that of Queen Caterina Cornaro at Asolo, while below the dense complex of grey-white walls and reddish tiled roofs it slopes away past the precipitous sides of the hill towards a landing-stage at the edge of a deep blue canal. The intimate narrative is unfolded with extraordinary naturalness, though its spirit is still informed with a classical measure of ideal beauty.

GIORGIONE (1476-1510), *The Tempest.* Oil on canvas (0,82-0,73) – c. 1507.

The vigour of cultural life at the beginning of the sixteenth century provided exactly the right fertile ground for the personality of Giorgione. With Giovanni Bellini and Vittore Carpaccio as examples in his early training and with his attentive interest in Northern European painting of Belgium he soon decided to attempt a naturalistic language. Colour attains to new, all-important powers of expression of the poetic equivalence of man and nature in a single, fearful apprehension of the cosmos. The finest of all expressions of this new vision of the world is the «Tempest», commissioned from the artist by Gabriele Vendramin, one of the leading lights in intellectual circles in the Venice of the day, in whose house the picture was recorded as having been hung by Marcantonio Michiel in 1530. Though many interpretations of the subject of this small painting have been suggested, none of them is totally convincing. Thus the mystery remains of what exactly the significance is of the fascinating landscape caught at this particular atmospheric moment, the breaking of a storm. Anxious waiting seems to characterize the mood of both the human figures, absorbed in private reveries, and

every other detail, from the little town half-hidden behind the luxuriant vegetation and the lazy, tortuous course of the stream to the ancient ruins, the houses, the towers and the buildings in the distance which pale against the blue of the sky. The fascination of the painting arises from the pictorial realization of the illustrative elements. In the vibrant brightness which immediately precedes the breaking of the storm the chromatic values follow one another in fluid gradations achieved by the modulation of the tones in the fused dialectic of light and shadow in an airy perspective of atmospheric value within a definite space. Completely liberated from any subjection to drawing or perspective, colour is the dominant value in a new spacial-atmospheric synthesis which is fundamental to the art of painting in its modern sense.

GIORGIONE, *The Old Woman.* Oil on canvas (0,68×0,59) – c. 1508.

The presentation of reality by means of a luminous medium which decants the subtlest gradations of colour with extraordinary fidelity and assembles them with immediacy into images of lyrical purity is a feature also of the extremely rare portraits by Giorgione, amongst them this painting of the «Old Woman». As with other pictures attributed with certainty to Giorgione hidden meanings have been searched for in the painting though the writing on the scroll – «col tempo» (with time) – would seem to suggest that its subject is the fading of beauty over the years. Despite the damage suffered by the painting, it is still possible to admire the freedom of touch, the mellow transparency of the medium with which the half figure of the woman is realized and the extraordinary realism with which her lost beauty is explored. The description of the shrivelled flesh, the aged eyelids, the toothless mouth, retains nothing at all of the Nordic prototypes and uses colour alone to create an objectively naturalistic image with consummate skill.

ROOMS 6, 7 and 8

(of the early sixteenth century)

In the first half of the sixteenth century several artists attempted to escape from the dominant taste established in Venetian painting by Giorgione and Titian. Lorenzo Lotto shut himself away in the jealous intimacy of his language, characterized by a restless mental sensibility; Girolamo Savoldo achieved a natural quality in his vigorous representations of reality; Girolamo Romanino added to the lessons learnt from the young Titian a fanciful expressionistic fervour; Alessandro Moretto applied himself to the search for reality with patient but somewhat dehumanising persistence; and Palma il Vecchio interpreted the sumptuousness of Titian's colour in effective, decorative terms. As the century moved towards its mid-point, artistic circles in Venice betrayed the influence of the anticlassical movement begun in Tuscany in the 1520s under the name of Mannerism. For a short time this new culture fascinated Titian too, and it certainly acted as a stimulus to the decorative elegance of Paris Bordone and to the narrative fluency of Bonifacio Veronese.

◆ **LORENZO LOTTO** (1480 c. – 1556), *Portrait of a Gentleman.* Oil on canvas (0,98×1,11) – c. 1525.

Coming originally from Bergamo, Lorenzo Lotto soon abandoned Venice in search of fresh artistic experience in other cities of the Veneto, in Lombardy, Rome and the Marches. He was influenced for example by Antonello da Messina, Melorro, Dürer, Raphael and Titian. In particular after his meditation on Lombard realism Lotto's painting, which never lent itself easily to rules of any kind, established an individual style based on a refined tension of compositional rhythms, a subtly natural light and a gentle blending of colours. Lotto's portraits achieve an extraordinary poetic quality and have a subtly autobiographical flavour about them with the at once melancholy and dreamy atmosphere which the subjects inhabit. One of the very finest of Lotto's portraits is this «Young Gentleman in his Study». The pale young man with his finely tapered face, is obviously a lover of both music and hunting, witness the mandola and the hunting horn hanging from the piece of furniture on the right, and is caught here in a moment of yearning thoughtfulness as his fingers leaf absent-mindedly through the pages of a large book. The natural light, entering through an invisible window, highlights the vibrant blacks and greys of his garments, the pale pink tones of his flesh and the blues of the table and just manages to penetrate the dark of the background in subdued illumination of the objects there, the finely turned ink-stand and the keys on the sideboard. The human figure too with its lack of any strong emotion, seems to participate in the arcane calm of this stupendous still life, the recently opened letter, the slow dropping of the rose petals, the silk shawl from whose folds darts a lizard. Such searching after human truth, veiled with melancholy, is at quite the opposite pole from the dignified idealization pursued by Titian in the portraits he painted at about the same time.

GIROLAMO SAVOLDO (1480 c. – 1550 c.), *St. Anthony Abbot and St. Paul.* Oil on canvas (1,65×1,37) – c. 1510.

Girolamo Savoldo was born in Brescia but spent a considerable amount of his life in Venice. His art is characterized by a realism derived from the Lombard masters in which several features of the broad nature of seventeenth century European painting are already present. An atmosphere of refined contemplation is the setting for his attempt to reconcile his leanings towards the culture of Lombardy with the sensitive lyricism of Giorgione and the eye for detail of the Flemish masters. A good example of this is the present «St. Anthony Abbot and St. Paul» in which the light shines from the right and glances off the figures, utterly human in their lifelike concreteness and completely alien to the canons of ideal beauty and perfect harmony obtained in the early sixteenth century.

GIROLAMO ROMANINO (1484/87-1566 c.), *Pietà.* Oil on panel (1,83×1,85) – 1510.

It is already clear in this, his first definitely dated work, that Girolamo Romanino, like Lotto and Savoldo, was reluctant to enter fully into the tradition of Venetian figurative art. The panel was painted for the Chapel of the Holy Passion in the old church of S. Lorenzo in Brescia and in it we can see Romanino's predilection for Titian's sonorously rich colour transposed onto a plane of popular narrative strengthened by a romantic, imaginative pathos. Against the background of a landscape which itself seems constricted in its atmosphere of profound anguish, the figures of the foreground seem to float to the surface in sharply cadenced groupings painted in timbres of a blazing quality. The influence of Lombard style which can be noted in the roundish faces painted after the fashion of Bramante, are accompanied by the influence of Northern European painting which can be seen in the view of the town glimpsed through the steamy, stormy atmosphere, in the objective quality of the portrait of the man, in the expressionistic deformation of the little human figures moving around the crosses at Golgotha. In this earliest attributable work by Romanino, the characteristic quality of the artist's style is already evident: an «expressionistic» realism which seems to offer an extremely personalized reflection of the political, social and religious crises that shook the Western world in the first half of the sixteenth century.

ALESSANDRO BONVICINO known as **MORETTO** (1498-1554), *The Virgin of Carmel.* Oil on canvas (2,71×2,98) – c. 1522.

Moretto was another painter influenced by Lombard naturalism but he preferred the intimate, muted study of reality characteristic of Foppa, Borgognone and Savoldo to the exuberant realism of Romanino. Among the greatest works of his youth can certainly be placed the «Virgin of Carmel» who is presented in the powerful and carefully gauged monumentally of a Madonna of Mercy with the figures of the Carmelites the Blessed Angelo and St. Simon Stock at her sides and a crowd of devotees below, probably members of the Brescian family the Ottoboni. The conspicuously earthly nature of the figures imparts to the celestial apparition a feeling of everyday reality, rendered with ineffable naturalness by the quiet light which defines poses, gestures, spiritual feelings themselves with such plastic objectivity. This «bourgeois» view of appearances marks the role of primary importance played by Moretto in Lombard «realism» which was to see Michelangelo Caravaggio as its greatest proponent around the end of the sixteenth century and the beginning of the seventeenth.

JACOPO PALMA IL VECCHIO (1480 c.-1528), *Sacred Conversation.* Oil on canvas (1,27×1,95) – c. 1525.

In contrast with Lotto, Savoldo, Romanino and Moretto, Jacopo Negretti, known as Palma il Vecchio, worked wholly within the tradition of Venetian painting. Influenced in his early years by the example of the great painters of the fifteenth century, he soon absorbed the lessons of Giorgione's revolution and subsequently fell under the spell of the personality of Titian, with the result that in his paintings of the early 1520s figures and landscape are both rendered in the most sumptuous of colours, both inhabit a calm, restful, sentimental atmosphere whose climate is unchanging and unchangeable. The masterpiece of this phase of his career is undoubtedly this «Sacred Conversation» which was perhaps the painting which Ridolfi quotes as hanging in the house of the Widmann family in 1648. The canvas reveals utter fidelity to Titian's style of around 1520, above all in the head of St. Catherine and the landscape with its castle which some critics believe was finished by Titian himself when the artist from Bergamo died and left some parts of the picture unfinished: for example, the left hand of St. Catherine and the right hand of St. John the Baptist. The spacious, monumental cadence of the rhythms of the figures offers the coloured passages the chance to spread in sumptuous zones defined by the polished refinement of his line, while shapes acquire a clean, plastic integrity through the effect of the limpid play of chiaroscuro. The opulent use of colour to bind the figures together gives clear evidence of Palma il Vecchio's propensity for the recreation of reality in an ideal model, unmoving and unmoved.

PARIS BORDONE (1500–1571), *The Presentation of the Ring.* Oil on canvas (3,70×3,01) – 1534.

After a phase of admiring study of Titian and Giorgione, Paris Bordone directed his attention first towards the impetuous art of Pordenone and then towards the intimistic narrative strength of the Brescians, to reach during the 1530s a brief period of equilibrium between sumptuousness of colour, inherited from Titian, and the adventurous freedom of composition learnt from the Mannerists. The universally recognized masterpiece of this period is the canvas Bordone painted in 1534 for the Hall of the Albergo in the Scuola Grande di San Marco. The subject of the picture is the second part of a legend which was very dear to Venetians. An old fisherman hands the Doge the ring given him by St. Mark as a proof of the help he gave the saint and two other patron saints of Venice, George and Nicholas, by taking them in his boat to the mouth of the lagoon at the Lido in order that they might make the sign of the cross to sink a boatful of demons that were on their way to threaten Venice with a terrible tempest. The naturalness of the scene, so rich in costumes, portraits and Lombardesque architecture, loses something of its intensity because of the theatrical nature of the architectural setting and because of the rhetorical quality of all the physical and spiritual reactions to the extraordinary event. Thus arises a sort of subtle uneasiness which spreads from the centre stage into the architectural wings of the scene and creates the impression of the rarified atmosphere of an event unrelated to time.

◆ **BONIFACIO DE' PITATI** known as **BONIFACIO VERONESE** (1487–1553), *Dives and Lazarus.* Oil on canvas (2,04×4,36) – 1540-50.

Like Paris Bordone, Bonifacio Veronese fails to convey the spiritual complexity of the world of the Mannerists, but used their formulae as a means of renewing and developing his innate gifts as a narrator. Thus he exploited the sensuous richness of the range of colours derived from Palma il Vecchio in his dynamic formal articulations and complex perspective-spacial proposals which were inspired in particular by prints of paintings by Raphael and the «Roman» artists. The most inspired poetic achievement of the fascinating decorative liberty attained by Bonifacio Veronese in the course of the fourth decade of the sixteenth century is without doubt this representation of «Dives and Lazarus» which is mentioned in 1660 by Boschini as hanging in Palazzo Giustiniani at San Stae. The Gospel parable is here not used as a prompt for dramatic effects but rather for the discursive presentation of a civilized meeting in the discreet half-light of the portico of a country house of the time. The languorous abandon to the music displayed by the group in the foreground is not in the least disturbed by the presence of the beggar, Lazarus, nor yet by the sudden bursting in of the armed men taking refuge from the fire blazing in the distance on the right, while the left and centre of the picture depict the serene passing of time in country house life: the servants intent on their bread-making, the lovers at the entrance to the tree garden, the hunters resting against the wall of the building. In the light, mellowed by the melancholy, yearning reflections of sunset, the colours acquire a refined neo-Byzantine richness and seem to be reminiscent of the «courtly» fables of Vittore Carpaccio.

TIZIANO VECELLIO (1488 c. – 1576), St. John the Baptist. Oil on canvas (2,01×1,34) – c. 1542.

Even more than in his «Presentation of the Virgin at the Temple», Titian's attempt to fill out his chromatic language with Mannerist elements is clearly evident in this «St. John the Baptist» painted for the now demolished church of Santa Maria Maggiore. The overpowering plasticity of the figure, its theatrical pose, and the strength of the timbres of the tones all reflect the dominant taste of the fifth decade of the sixteenth century in a Venice which was increasingly concerned with the problems of form and composition that preoccupied the «classicists» of Central Italy, ideas that were propagated in Venice by Jacopo Sansovino, Vasari and Salviati. But even in this muscular athlete (certainly no hermit emaciated by exhausting fasts) the formal academic quality of Mannerism is redeemed by Titian's sensitivity to colour: the «impasto» of the paint seems almost to be rising in the luminous matching of the grey of the skin to the ivory colour of the flesh and in the browns, greens and darkened by the rushing torrent. Indeed it was precisely because of his feeling for colour that in Titian the formulae of Mannerism, instead of crystalizing in abstract programmatic projects, was translated into an enthusiasm for research.

ROOMS 10 and 11 (of Titian, Tintoretto and Paolo Veronese)

(first part)

These two magnificent rooms were constructed between 1821 and 1825 to the designs of Antonio Selva to house the growing collection of the Galleries. Now they are dedicated to Titian, Jacopo Tintoretto and Paolo Veronese, the three great masters of painting in Venice during the second half of the sixteenth century. At the end of his long life, after a career which saw him constantly engaged in new research, Titian achieved a magic chromatic alchemy in which his cosmic, tragic vision of the world remains manifestly linked to the Renaissance conception. At the same time Jacopo Tintoretto's luminism which grew out of the traditions of Mannerism, takes the form of an intense, popular religiosity which seems to herald the Baroque age. Paolo Veronese on the other hand is quite indifferent to the spiritual concerns of Mannerism, and instead celebrates, in a hymn of dazzling brightness and Olympian confidence, the glory and «joie de vivre» of sixteenth century Venice.

GIOVANNI ANTONIO DE' SACCHIS known as **PORDENONE** (1483/84-1539), *St. Lorenzo Giustiniani and other Saints.* Oil on canvas (4,20×2,20) - 1532.

Born in Friuli, Pordenone underwent his early training as a painter in an artistic context still heavily influenced by Mantegna, but subsequently he experienced a multiplicity of different fashions and styles in Venice, Ferrara, Loreto, Rome and Urbino where he came into contact with Giorgione, Titian, Sebastiano del Piombo, Melozzo da Forlì, Raphael and Michelangelo. The taste which arose from this wide-ranging education was marked by an expressive mannerist vitality that found itself in conflict in Venice with the courtly classicism of Titian. Such expressive passion loses some of its intensity in the later phase of Pordenone's career and under the refined Mannerist influence of Parmigiano his figure groupings became more studied and tightly organized. It is to this last period of Pordenone's activity that the great altar-piece of St. Lorenzo Giustiniani belongs, with the saint pictured standing between two «fratelli turchini» and St. Francis and St. Augustine on the left and St. Bernardino and St. John the Baptist on the right. The work was completed in 1532 for the Church of Madonna dell'Orto where the Canons of S. Giorgio in Alga (the «fratelli turchini», so-called because of the blue-green colour of their vestments) celebrated mass. In the play of light and shade achieved with considerable dramatic tension by means of the circular sky-light in the architectural structure, the figures of the saints are presented as a magnificent series of interlocking shapes, a dense interweaving of sentiments.

JACOPO TINTORETTO (1518-1594), *The Miracle of St. Mark freeing the slave.* Oil on canvas (4,15×5,41) – 1548.

By 1539 the young Jacopo Tintoretto had already set up an independent studio. He experimented with styles of painting different from that of Titian and came under the influence of the Tuscan-Roman Mannerist tradition, drawing on the robust, luminous plasticity of Pordenone, the narrative fluency of Bonifacio Veronese, Michelangelo's use of chiaroscuro, Parmigianino's supple linearism as well as the pictorial plasticity of Jacopo Sansovino. Tintoretto's imagination used every suggestion to create a dramatic scenographic language which in his early works achieves moments of pure poetry, such as in the «Miracle of St. Mark freeing the slave», the first of a series of works, painted in 1548 for the Scuola Grande di S. Marco while Marco Episcopi, his future father-in-law, was Grand Guardian of the School. The subject of the huge canvas is the miraculous appearance of St. Mark to rescue one of his devotees, a servant of a knight of Provence, who had been condemned to having his legs broken and his eyes put out for worshipping the relics of the saint against his master's will. The scene takes place on a kind of proscenium which seems to force the action out of the painting towards the spectator who is thus involved in the amazement of the crowd standing in a semi-circle around the protagonists: the fore-shortened figure of the slave lying on the ground, the dumbfounded executioner holding aloft the broken implements of torture, the knight of Provence starting up from his seat out of the shadow into the light, while the figure of St. Mark swoops down from above. In keeping with the drama of the action is the tight construction of the painting, the dramatic foreshortening of the forms and the sudden strong contrast of light and shade. The vibrant colour also enforces the dramatic theme by changing restlessly under the invisible spotlights which light up the foreground while the background appears to be in natural daylight.

JACOPO TINTORETTO, *Creation of the animals.* Oil on canvas (1,51×2,58) – c. 1550.

One of the major achievements of Tintoretto's early works is the series of canvases painted in about 1550 for the Sala dell'Albergo of the Scuola della Santissima Trinità. And of these the «Creation of the animals» is certainly unique for the swirling rhythm of the composition. In a blaze of golden light, which does not entirely escape the darkness still partly enveloping the newly created earth, God the Father is portrayed as if suspended in mid-air in the act of creation. The animals rush forward from behind him while the birds shoot across the sky and the fishes dart through the water like arrows from his hand. The dramatic wind-swept scene is furrowed by the profiles of the animals which cross the canvas in running lines, conveying with extraordinary concision and expressiveness the theme of the work.

JACOPO TINTORETTO, *Adam and Eve*. Oil on canvas (1,50×2,20) – c. 1550.

Adam and Eve are depicted not in a landscape thrown into confusion by the hand of the Creator but in a more serene, more human dimension. In the leafy arbour the two nude figures moving around the trunk of the tree form the parallel diagonals of the composition. A strong light gives a sculptural effect to their ivory-pink flesh. But in the background, on the right, the tranquillity of the foreground scene gives way to the tumultuous epilogue to the fact of human disobedience to Divine will. With rapid brushstrokes Tintoretto evokes the fiery angel who drives Adam and Eve out into the distant desolate hills and plains.

➡ **JACOPO TINTORETTO**, *St. Jerome and St. Andrew*. Oil on canvas (2,25×1,45) – c. 1552.

The works of Tintoretto after the middle of the 16th century demonstrate still more clearly the search for strong sculptural effects achieved by use of chiaroscuro, a complex scenographic spatial representation and the use of clear, bright colour in direct contrast to the more subdued harmonies of Titian's «magica alchimia cromatica». The work «St. Jerome and St. Andrew» is a major example of these tendencies. It was commissioned for one of the rooms of the Magistrato del Sale in the Palazzo dei Camerlenghi at Rialto by Andrea Dandolo and Girolamo Bernardo, magistrates who left office between September and October 1552. The search for a Manneristic figural rhythm within the overall compositional plan is evident. The figure of St. Andrew takes up the whole of the small space to the left of the cross, leaving more room for St. Jerome alongside the curvilinear outline of the rock. The scenic effect of the figures constrained in a small space is given unity and the poetic sense of an intense spiritual life by the expressive force of light which brings out all the gradations of colour.

JACOPO TINTORETTO, *St. Louis, St. George and the Princess*. Oil on canvas (2,26×1,46) – c. 1553. ➡

This work, commissioned by Giorgio Venier and Alvise Foscarini who left the Magistratura del Sale respectively on September 13th 1551 and May 10th 1553, is a fine example of Tintoretto's achievement of a dynamic compositional tension. The incisive force of the line combines with rich and luminous colour to create the firmly modelled figures. The self-conscious statement of dramatic style became another pretext for the continuing polemic between Tintoretto and Titian. Dolce clearly alludes to it when, in his «Dialogo della pittura» of 1558, he criticizes the unfortunate position of the princess, whom he takes to be St. Margaret, astride the dragon.

JACOPO TINTORETTO, *The stealing of the body of St. Mark*. Oil on canvas (3,98×3,15) – 1562.

In 1562 Jacopo Tintoretto was commissioned by the Guardian Grande, Tommaso Ragnone, to complete the decoration of the School of St. Mark. This work relates the episode in which the Christians of Alexandria, taking advantage of a sudden hurricane, take possession of the body of the saint which was about to be burned by the pagans. The group in the foreground (where Ragnone himself is depicted bearing the head of the saint) stands out sculpturally from the vertiginous depth of the background created by use of light and by the obsessive architectural sequence of arcades and mullioned windows which terminate in the phosphorescence of the Sanmichelilike construction outlined against a reddish sky heavy with clouds. Light assumes an elemental role in this phantasmagorical graphic scene, bestowing on every detail an extraordinary impression of movement.

JACOPO TINTORETTO, *St. Mark saving a Saracen from shipwreck.* Oil on canvas (3,98×3,37) – 1562.

This scene depicts the episode in which Saint Mark, according to legend, saved the life of a Saracen, his secret follower, by restoring him to the boat from which he had been thrown by the Christians during a storm at sea. The figures form a diagonal which is continually broken to indicate the fury of the natural elements. The stormy sea and wind-tossed clouds evoke the meteorological conditions in a way which is almost over-dramatized. This is, however, a superb example of the visionary and fantastical style of Tintoretto, who uses light to convey the desired appearance of reality.

TIZIANO VECELLIO (TITIAN) (c. 1488-1576), *Pietà*. Oil on canvas (3,52×3,49) – 1576.

In the second half of the 16th century Titian was continually overburdened with commissions for work – from Charles V and Philip II, from the Republic and from many churches. Overcoming the crisis of Mannerism shortly before his stay in Rome at the Papal court (1545/6), Titian's work now took on a new incomparable coherence of vision and creative force. We witness the triumph of colour and light over the Renaissance notions of sculptural form. In his later works Titian's handling of colour is suffused with spirituality; his youthful themes lose their Phidian serenity and from the burning

rhythm of interwoven tones which melt slowly into the glowing tints images emerge, at times dramatic, at times full of emotion for lost earthly happiness. In his Pietà, originally planned for his tomb at the Frari and left unfinished at his death, Titian achieves the high point of the expressive possibilities of his «alchimia cromatica». The work was completed by Palma il Giovane who added the torch-bearing cherub. The opaque density of this detail contrasts with the «magical impressionism» of Titian's tonal harmonies. In the shimmering nocturnal scene figures of flesh and marble are evoked by a suffusion of glowing colour. And along the diagonal formed by the figures we are witness to an outpouring of human passion: Mary Magdalene turns in a cry of uncontrollable grief, the Virgin appears frozen in contemplation of her dead son and St. Jerome leans forward to catch the last breath of Christ.

PAOLO CALIARI (known as **VERONESE**) (1528-1588), *Madonna enthroned with saints*. Oil on canvas (3,39×1,91) – c. 1562.

Paolo Veronese left his native Verona in 1553 to settle in Venice where he came under the influence of the Venetian figurative tradition and then Mannerism, in particular of Parmigianino and Giulio Romano. The rich and complex arrangement of his compositions is matched by a brilliant use of colour, characterized by the juxtaposition of complementary colours and a vibrant solar light. The «Virgin enthroned and child with saints» was painted for the Sacristy of S. Zaccaria (restored in 1562) is a fine example of the early works of Veronese with its harmonious richness of colour. The young John the Baptist stands at the meeting point of the two compositional diagonals formed by the figures of St. Joseph, St. Francis and St. Jerome, who are invested with a look of detached spirituality. The colour is made vibrant by a continual juxtaposition of light and dark tones. Through an understanding of the interaction of colour every hue is intensified and enriched. The diapason of Veronesian colour is achieved in the portrayal of the Virgin and child set against the damask of the niche.

PAOLO VERONESE, *Feast in the House of Levi*. Oil on canvas (5,55×12,80) – 1573.

This work painted for the Dominican order of SS. Giovanni e Paolo to replace an earlier work by Titian destroyed in the fire of 1571, is the last of the grandiose «suppers» painted by Veronese for the refectories of Venetian monasteries. The sumptuous banquet scene is framed by the great arches of a portico. Against the pale green shotsilk effect of the background architecture, the figures on either side of Christ move in a turbulence of polychromatic splendour and interaction of pose and gesture. We seem to see here the sublime notions of form and colour of Piero della Francesca. The interaction of form and colour is calculated to contain the monumental figuration within the terms of a fascinating

and imaginative decorative painting. The expressive hedonism so alien to the religious context – the subject in fact appears to be a purely pagan one in exaltation of the love of life in 16th century Venice – aroused the suspicions of the Inquisition. On July 18th 1573 Veronese was summoned by the Holy Office to appear before the Inquisition accused of heresy. If the questions of the inquisitors show the first signs of the rigours of the Counter-reformation, Veronese's answers show clearly his unfailing faith in the creative imagination and in artistic freedom. Not wishing to yield to the injunction of the Inquisition to eliminate the details which offended the religious theme of the Last Supper, he changed the title to «Feast in the house of Levi», a subject which tolerated the presence of fools and armed men dressed up «alla todesca».

PAOLO VERONESE, *The marriage of St. Catherine*. Oil on canvas (3,37×2,41) – c. 1575.

In this work, originally the altar-screen of the church of St. Catherine, Veronesian colour reaches a peak of richness and splendour. Along the diagonal of the composition which terminates in the drapes billowing around the columns, new chromatic notes are struck; the «fortissimo» of the steps and figures in the foreground harmonizes with the «pianissimo» of angels and cherubs which emerge from the grey-gold clouds of the celestial kingdom in the background. Linking the two planes of colour are two cherubs holding the martyr's palm and the heavenly crown above the Virgin and St. Catherine while the angel below lifts her head and holds out her arms to receive the sign and the reward of martyrdom. All three are portrayed with Apollonian purity against the intense blue of the sky, an unforgettable example of Veronese's exquisite use of colour. Even more appropriate is the 17th century comment by Marco Boschini: «It is almost as if the painter to create his effects used gold, pearls and rubies, emeralds, sapphires and purest, most perfect diamonds».

PAOLO VERONESE, *Battle of Lepanto*. Oil on canvas (1,69×1,37) – c. 1562.

This small painting, originally placed on the left of the altar of the Rosary in the church of St. Peter Martyr on Murano, is probably an ex-voto commissioned by Pietro Giustinian of Murano who took part in the naval battle at Lepanto on October 7th 1561 when the Turkish fleet was defeated thanks mainly to the Venetian ships. The play of tone and light in the lower part depicting the battle is masterly. In the top part, above a curtain of cloud, the Saints Peter, Roch, Justine and Mark implore the Virgin to grant victory to the Christian fleet. In answer to this an angel hurls burning arrows at the Turkish vessels.

PAOLO VERONESE, *Ceres renders homage to Venice*. Oil on canvas (3,09×3,28) – 1575.

This painting, which dates from 1575, originally decorated the ceiling of the Magistrato delle Biade in the Doge's Palace. In the skilful perspective and in the limpid intensity of tone the figures stand out against the blue sky broken by white-gold clouds, achieving a perfect balance in space with a rhythmic natural elegance and olimpian beauty. Even the figures in half-light are endowed with the same intense luminous colour. The figure of Venice enthroned is of particular beauty.

PAOLO VERONESE, *The people of Myra welcoming St. Nicholas*. Oil on canvas (1,98 diametre) – c. 1582.

Towards the end of his life Paolo Veronese's creative imagination becomes veiled with an inner poetry. His colours no longer stand out in brilliant juxtapositions but become more modulated with rich effects of light and shade. This work, one of seven painted for the ceiling of the church of S. Nicolo della Lattuga which was consecrated in 1582, belongs to this period. Damaged at the sides, only the central part of the composition remains. Two groups of figures form the two parallel diagonals, one coming forward, the other with St. Nicholas held back. The subtlety of the Veronesian palette is as ever remarkable for the variation of tone, here used to create a naturalistic effect.

ROOM 11 (Tiepolo)

(second part)

Even if it is not the greatest of the five centuries of Venetian painting represented in the Academy Galleries, the 17th century is not without interesting artists (cf. p. 62-65). One of these, the Genoese Bernardo Strozzi brought with him to Venice a fondness for the sensual richness of colour gained from a familiarity with the works of Barocci, with Gentileschi and Borgianni who were influenced by Caravaggio, and with Rubens and Van Dyck. A further stimulus to the revival of Venetian art in the second half of the 17th century was the presence there of the Neapolitan Luca Giordano whose artistic language with its atmospheric luminosity anticipates the new freer use of colour in 18th century Venetian painting (cf. p. 66-70). Artist of both the sacred and profane history of 18th century Venice and Europe Giambattista Tiepolo achieves in his sketches and small paintings moments of lyricism and intimate poetry, while the grandiloquent style of his great decorative works sings the praises, at times with an ironic note, of the grandiose myths of the time.

LUCA GIORDANO, *Crucifixion of St. Peter.* Oil on canvas (1,96×2,58) – c. 1660.

Coming from the «naturalist» studio of the Spaniard Giuseppe Ribera, follower of Caravaggio, the Neapolitan Luca Giordano was also influenced by the Roman Baroque artists as well as by the Venetian 16th century painters. His fluid, luminous style anticipates the development of Venetian painting in the 18th century. In this work the rhythmic articulations of the composition around the cross of St. Peter and the smoky colour which seems to fuse in the golden light combine to create an effect of continual movement and intense realism.

◀ **BERNARDO STROZZI** (1581-1644), *Banquet at the house of Simon.* Oil on canvas (2,72×7,42) – c. 1629.

Bernardo Strozzi, the last of the three painters who revitalized Venetian painting at the beginning of the 17th century, came to Venice from Genoa in 1631. In his works the artistic language of Fetti and Liss (cf. p. 74-76) is developed in a more decorative style influenced by Veronese, with a robust exuberance of colour reminiscent of Rubens. Strozzi's admiration for Veronese even before leaving Genoa is evident in «Banquet at the house of Simon», clearly inspired by the works of the great painter, even if the exuberant style is now clearly Baroque. The banquet table is set diagonally in the wide niche. There are two focal points to the composition: Christ defending Mary Magdalene and Simon leaning incredulously over the table. A dense, rich colour, vibrant with atmospheric luminosity renders the figures physically and spiritually alive. The close observation of detail has a post-Caravaggio realism in the brilliant depiction of the servant interrupting the scuffle between a dog and a cat, or of the page bearing a tray of fruit, silhouetted against the sky.

GIAMBATTISTA TIEPOLO (1696-1770), *The scourge of the serpents* (fragment). Oil on canvas (1,64×13,56) – 1732–35.

During the 1720s Giambattista Tiepolo developed a new colouristic style of painting, derived in principle from the dazzling palette of Veronese and the no less brilliant one of Sebastiano Ricci (cf. p. 66). Rejecting the tenebrous colour of Piazzetta (cf. p. 85), we witness in Tiepolo the triumph of colour with a richness of resonance and counterpoint elaborated within the ordered and monumental composition. The great frieze, originally below the choir of the Venetian church of SS. Cosma and Damiani on the Giudecca (Zanetti 1771), is a fine example of Tiepolo's work of the 1730s. The painting in its ornate stucco frame decorated with fruit, flowers and leaves is over 13 metres long. Three episodes are depicted with a decorative illusionism contrasting with the declared realist-narrative intent, rendering the painting somewhat melodramatic in effect.

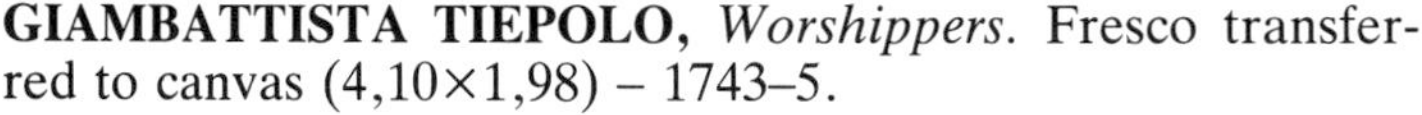

GIAMBATTISTA TIEPOLO, *Worshippers.* Fresco transferred to canvas (4,10×1,98) – 1743–5.

Giambattista Tiepolo collaborated with the Venetian quadratura painter, Girolamo Mengozzi Colonna on the ceiling fresco of the nave of the church of St. Mary of Nazareth called the «Scalzi», completing the work in 1743-45 following the careful preparation of studies and models (cf. p. 87). The grandiose fresco depicting the «transportation of the holy house of Loreto» was almost completely destroyed during World War I. The few remaining fragments, such as this «Worshippers», are enough to evoke the richness of colour and conception of this major decorative achievement. The silver-white tones of the visionary shrine are illuminated by the dazzling hues of the garments of the nobleman who looks up towards the saintly apparition while his servant glances curiously downward towards the crowded nave.

GIAMBATTISTA TIEPOLO, *Discovery of the true Cross.* Oil on canvas (4,90 diam.) – c. 1745.

This grandiose tondo, originally the centrepiece of the ceiling decorated by Girolamo Mengozzi Colonna in the Capuchin church in Castello, is a typical example of Tiepolo's ability to translate any theme, sacred or profane into a stupendous Baroque magniloquence. Within the monumental order the areas of colour are arranged in patterns of polychromatic splendour, suffused with a pure light which highlights every carefully observed detail. In this remarkable example of illusionistic perspective, with which Tiepolo never tired of amazing his contemporaries, the images are characterized by distinct notes of colours and emotion with a fascinating musical decorative freshness.

ROOM 12

(18 th century landscape painting)

In much of the long corridor above the surviving wing of the Cloister, which was part of the monastery of S. Maria della Carità, designed in 1561 by Andrea Palladio, is a collection of Venetian 18th century landscape paintings. Originator of the genre was Marco Ricci, who painted his native land with a dramatic imagination and romantic fantasy. Giuseppe Zaîs interprets the master's themes and poetry with a kind of rustic grace. The paintings of Francesco Zuccarelli, however, depict an ideal pastoral landscape; with his easy light-hearted style he achieves a lyrical portrayal of a rose-tinted world.

MARCO RICCI (1679-1729), *Landscape with horses.* Oil on canvas (1,36×1,98) – c. 1720; *Landscape with river and figures* (fragment). Oil on canvas (1,37×1,98) – c. 1720.

If Sebastiano Ricci can be called the father of Venetian Rococo (cf. p. 81), his nephew and collaborator, Marco, was the initiator of the new genre of landscape painting. Influenced by the examples of the Neapolitan landscape painters Mirco Spadaro and Salvator Rosa, by Claude Lorrain and by the Roman Viviano Codazzi, and inspired by loving observation of the natural setting of hills and valleys around his native Belluno, Ricci developed a romantic and heroic style of painting, which derives almost certainly from a familiarity with the drawings of Titian, the engravings of Domenico Campagnola, the works of Dutch and Flemish masters (seen during his stay in London 1708-10), with the imaginative works of Carlevaris and romantic drama of Alessandro Magnasco (cf. p. 81). Such eclecticism gives rise nevertheless to a faithful observation of nature, characterized by a breadth of atmosphere and a fluid light. These two landscapes are fine examples of his skilful use of light to create intensely real effects. In the wide vistas given unity by Ricci's handling of atmosphere, the observation of detail has a refreshing naturalness and truth.

FRANCESCO ZUCCARELLI (1702-1788), *Bacchanal.* Oil on canvas (1,42×2,10) – 1740-50; *The rape of Europa* (fragment). Oil on canvas (1,42×2,08) – 1740-50.

The Tuscan painter Francesco Zuccarelli came to Venice in 1732. He was familiar with trends in European painting, having visited London and Paris. His ideal pastoral landscapes are characterized by an arcadian grace in the use of colour, by a harmonious rhythm of gesture, a softness of tone and a hazy atmosphere filling the spacious vistas. In the idyllic countryside, pastoral or mythological scenes are set against a brilliant green or water-side background. The paintings are sentimental, sometimes achieving a refined lyricism in keeping with the light-hearted ideals of the time.

GIUSEPPE ZAIS (1709-1784), *Landscape with ruins and archway*. Oil on canvas (0,97×1,47) – 1730; *Landscape with river and bridge*. Oil on canvas (0,97×1,43) – c. 1740.

The early landscapes of Giuseppe Zais, are similar in style to those of his master and fellow-countryman, Marco Ricci. In the grandiose «Ruins and archway» a dramatic pictorial quality is achieved by the use of strong chiaroscuro effects. In the 1740s his rustic scenes acquire a simplicity and sincerity more like the pastoral scenes of Zuccarelli with their more light-hearted themes and softer colour. «Landscape with river and bridge» is a fine example of the balance of colour and atmosphere achieved by Zais in his works of this period.

ROOM 13

(Jacopo Bassano)

If, around the middle of the 16th century, many Venetian artists such as Paris Bordone, Bonifacio Veronese (cf. p. 45-47) and Andrea Schiavone, flirted with the formal elements of Mannerism, Jacopo Bassano can be said to have embraced it whole-heartedly, only to then turn his back on it in favour of a style more concerned with figural rhythm and limpid colour quite distinct from the subdued tones of Titian. Unlike the sterile Mannerist style, his use of form and colour has a vitality of expression and lyric striking intensity. His later works have an everyday realism which anticipates the trends of the 17th century.

ANDREA MELDOLLA known as **SCHIAVONE** (1500/10-1563), *The judgement of Midas.* Oil on panel (0,40×1,18) – c. 1550.

Even more so than his master Bonifacio Veronese (cf. p. 47), Andrea Schiavone was influenced by Mannerist styles of painting especially that of Parmigianino, whose refined conceptual elegance becomes in the works of Schiavone a liberating freedom of rhythm which is both decorative and sensuous. But, as we see in this small panel, his sensitive fluency of composition has little of the dynamic metaphysical vitality of Parmigianino.

JACOPO DA PONTE known as **BASSANO** (1510/19-1592), *St. Jerome.* Oil on canvas (1,19×1,54) – 1556.

Although he worked mainly in his native Bassano (from where he gets his name), away from the main artistic centres, Jacopo Bassano played an active role in the cultural life of the time. Pupil of Bonifacio Veronese and student of Titian, Pordenone, Lorenzo Lotto and Savoldo, and an admirer of German engravings, he was inspired by Mannerism and by Parmigianino in particular. He developed and refined a style where a polished use of colour turns Mannerist preciosity into an extreme realist representation, achieving in his later works a sensibility which prefigures the 17th century. The striking naturalism of «St. Jerome» belongs to the beginning of this late period. The saint is portrayed in meditation in the cave which was his refuge and behind which we can glimpse on the right the rain-swept countryside. The livid autumn twilight highlights with realistic truth every vein and wrinkle of the body consumed by a life of privation and picks out the details of the objects on the ground: the hour-glass, the leather-bound volumes, the skull rolled into the shadow. The rare patches of colour pulsate with a shimmering brightness in the play of light and shadow on the dark brown of the rock, conveying the everyday truth of the melancholy of the place and the time of day. The expressive freedom of colour and effects of light inspired El Greco during his formative years in Venice although the artistic visions of the two painters were very different. In fact, for Bassano effects of colour and light are essential to achieve a material reality, while for El Greco they are the fundamental elements of his stunning abstract precepts.

JACOPO TINTORETTO, *Portrait of Jacopo Soranzo.* Oil on canvas (1,06×0,89) – c. 1550.

This fine example of Tintoretto's portraits is a fragment of a larger work which contains other portraits and dates from not long after the other portrayal of Jacopo Soranzo in the possession of the Castello Sforzesco in Milan. No longer governed by precepts of Renaissance portraiture, this painting exemplifies an immediacy of interpretation and a penetrating understanding of the psychology of the sitter. In the portrait of Soranzo the brush strokes build up the features of the face with extraordinary precision, subtle effects of light evoking the leanness of the flesh, the burning eyes, the hair and beard of the subject. A sudden light forces Soranzo out of the shadow and he appears to be engaged in an intense conversation with the observer, revealing to him his innermost human and spiritual emotions. The rapid «expressionistic» way in which the character is conveyed is very different from the idealized dignity which Titian confers upon his powerful contemporaries in his portraits of them.

JACOPO PALMA IL GIOVANE (1544-1628), *The Crucifixion of St. Peter.* Oil on canvas (1,68×1,32) – c. 1590.

The four great artists working in Venice in the second half of the sixteenth century, Titian, Jacopo Tintoretto, Paolo Veronese and Jacopo Bassano, had no local followers of any great significance. Minor artists did try to reproduce the works of the inimitable masters, but their attempts inevitably failed and they achieved no more than an academic mannerism. Even Palma il Giovane, the leading exponent of Venetian «Mannerism» towards the end of the century, does not entirely escape this criticism. He worked for a long time with Titian but preferred a simple version of Tintoretto's luminous style to Titian's «chromatic magic». The «Crucifixion of St. Peter also betrays the influence of Tintoretto. The division of the canvas into three parts gives rise to a distinctly balanced compositional rhythm: Paradise and the Holy Trinity at the top, the crucifixion of St. Peter below and on the right in the background, the beheading of St. Paul.

ROOM 14

(of the seventeenth century)

In the early years of the sixteen hundreds the stagnant waters of Venetian artistic culture were stirred by the presence of Fetti, Liss and Strozzi who brought to Venice an echo of some of the greatest painters of seventeenth century Europe, of Caravaggio and Rubens in particular. The vivid, sparkling style of Fetti, the brilliance and free and easiness of Liss and the sensual exuberance of Strozzi were all fundamental influences on the two most important representatives of seventeenth century baroque in Venice, Francesco Maffei and Sebastiano Mazzoni, the first an emphatic, fanciful colourist whose style verges on the grotesque, and the second a fertile source of fluid, stylizing ideas which are supported by a subtle intellectual commitment.

DOMENICO FETTI (1589-1623), *David* (detail). Oil on canvas (1,75×1,28) – c. 1620.

After early training in the studios of followers of Caravaggio in Rome, Domenico Fetti moved to Mantua in 1614. Here he came into contact with the exuberant painting of Rubens and with masterpieces of the great sixteenth century Venetian artists. Thus he began to work within the cultural ambit of Venice and after a first visit there in 1621 he returned to settle in the city in the following year. This «David» belongs to the Mantua years and is an excellent example of the fresh, lively freedom of invention of Fetti. The sensuality of the colours and the skilful placing of the figure prevail over the inky darkness of the shadows. And the young cavalier, as he places the symbols of his iconographical identity in the shadows, offers himself to the light resplendent in the brilliantly colourful tokens of his rank and his era: the red plumed cap placed boldly on his head, the downy collar and his olive-green jacket with its fashionable slashed sleeves.

DOMENICO FETTI, *Parable of the Good Samaritan.* Oil an canvas (0,61×0,45) – c. 1623.

When Fetti came into contact with Paolo Veronese's clear, luminous colours on his arrival in Venice, his delicate naturalism, which clearly owed a lot to Caravaggio, took a richer turn and he found an ideal vehicle for his airy, unrestrained inventiveness in paintings of small dimensions such as the celebrated «parables». In the «Parable of the Good Samaritan» in the collection of the Accademia Galleries the gospel story is used (even more so than in the previous version in the collections of the Gemälde-galerie of Dresden, the Metropolitan Museum of New York and Boston Museum) as a pretext for a skilful, rapid setting of a natural everyday scene caught in the lyrically evoked moment of sunset.

DOMENICO FETTI, *The Meditation.* Oil on canvas (1,79×1,40) – c. 1623.

Fetti dealt also with the larger allegorical themes with captivating naturalness. In this «Meditation» for example, which clearly alludes to the vanity of earthly things. The interplay of light and shade on the subject (the female figure gazing pensively at the skull for example) gives rise to a sense of abandonment, of anxious melancholy. And every detail in the recess of the courtyard seems to assume a material consistency with the vine growing out of the rough surface of the wall perhaps the most beautiful of all.

GIOVANNI LISS (1595 c.-1629), *Apollo and Marsyas*. Oil on canvas (0,58×0,48) – c. 1627.

The early training of Liss took place in Amsterdam under Hendrik Goltzius who painted very much in the style of the Italian Mannerists. After attending school in Haarlem, he spent two years in Rome as part of the circle of Flemish artists linked by their admiration of Caravaggio. In 1624 he moved to Venice. All his artistic means, which had once been brilliant and sensual, were now aiming for an effect of hazy vagueness and already seemed to offer a foretaste of the Rococo age. A good example from the very limited output of Liss is «Apollo and Marsyas» where the cruel event of the Greek mythological subject fades into a feeling of silent, panic-stricken excitement.

GIOVANNI LISS, *Abel mourned by his parents*. Oil on canvas (0,67×0,84) – c. 1628.

In the paintings of Liss there is always a vivid sense of the landscape participating in the human events it frames. In «Abel mourned by his parents» the fierce glow of the setting sun casts reddish reflections on the sky, against which stand out two poplar trees and Adam and Eve grieving over the lifeless body of their son in the deepening half-light on the side of the barren hill.

GIULIO CARPIONI (1613-1674), *Crucifixion*. Oil on canvas (2,05×1,31) – c. 1648.

Giulio Carpioni was initially a pupil of Alessandro Varotari, known as «Il Padovanino», who, in the early years of the seventeenth century, had reacted to the mortifying conformism of the late Mannerists by returning to the classicism of the young Titian for his inspiration. Carpioni subsequently refined the intentions of his master still further in a sort of ideal classic style through the polished sharpness of his line and the cold, brilliant range of colours he used. In his «Crucifixion» the devotional aims are conveyed through an atmosphere of abstract, formal severity.

I N R I

FRANCESCO MAFFEI (1600 c.-1660), *Perseus cuts the Medusa's head off.* Oil on canvas (1,30×1,61) – c. 1650.

After studying in Vicenza under Maganza, a late Mannerist painter of limited importance, Francesco Maffei turned to the paintings of Tintoretto, Paolo Veronese and Jacopo Bassano and soon achieved a personal style based on a Baroque reworking of the lessons taught by the great artists of the sixteenth century. Maffei moved to Venice in 1638, was attracted by the painters Liss, Fetti and Strozzi and developed his own version of their free and fanciful modern painting with a gifted, exuberant dreamlike quality. Amongst the most significant examples of this period is the painting of «Perseus cutting the head off the Medusa». The figures, painted with impetuous, disdainful passion, crowd on the surface of the picture and are completely lacking in perspective relationship and in precise setting in their surroundings. The bright tones seem to swell as if as the result of some internal pressure, offering themselves as incandescent magma to the light which breaks them up into iridescent chromatic ornamental units. The sensual brightness of the colours underlines the emphatic strain on the links between the figures, lending the whole an emotional theatricality which was amongst the most visionary and unbiassed of the Baroque age in Venice.

SEBASTIANO MAZZONI (1611 c.-1678), *Annunciation.* Oil on canvas (2,26×1,57) – c. 1650.

The Florentine artist Sebastiano Mazzoni, who was a poet and architect as well as a painter, rivals Francesco Maffei as the most lively and imaginative painter of the Baroque period in Venice. Under the influence of Fetti, Liss and above all Strozzi, Mazzoni aimed for a style of airily elegant images moving in a space with which he could experiment ex novo in freely imaginative terms. His early training in Tuscany did however remain influential with the result that in Mazzoni the decorative exuberance of Maffei seems to be passed through an intellectual filter even in the bolder examples of figure painting. In the «Annunciation», the angel bends over the Virgin who is depicted humbly accepting the divine message. Against the architectural background, the two figures spread over the limited space, while their colours are of the most refined. This lyrical evocation of reality through highly coloured facets dissolved into the atmosphere in dancing rhythms was to be completely understood only in the eighteenth century.

ROOMS 15, 16, 16a and 17 (of the eighteenth century)

Venetian painting in the eighteenth century looked once again towards the wider horizons of Europe. Sebastiano Ricci, Giannantonio Pellegrini and Jacopo Amigoni have a place amongst the greatest representatives of international Rococo, and were amongst the most authoritative propagators of that evanescent and delicate world in Italy and Europe. Beside their works, sparkling and airy and almost completely lacking in serious spiritual intentions, we have the expressive intensity of the paintings of Giambattista Piazzetta, at first marked by a considerable use of chiaroscuro and subsequently radiant with a «lume solivo». It was at this intensity of expression that Giambattista Tiepolo aimed initially, and with his grandiose scenographical undertakings (cf. p. 86-87) he soon became the symbol of the century in the field of the depiction of sacred and profane history. Together with the great decorative paintings, other «genres» of paintings developed: the landscape, originated by the brilliant Marco Ricci (cf. p. 66); the domestic scenes of contemporary society, registered with goodhumoured grace by Pietro Longhi and with incomparable psychological penetrative force by Rosalba Carriera; the view, objectively lucid in Canaletto and romantically evocative in Francesco Guardi. Thus, with a whole range of different voices, the great five century long arc of Venetian painting drew to a close.

FRANCESCO SOLIMENA (1657-1743), *Rebecca and Eleazar.* Oil on canvas (2,02×1,50) – c. 1710.

Francesco Solimena was greatly admired by the Venetian painters of the eighteenth century, especially by Piazzetta and the young Giambattista Tiepolo, for his vigorous naturalism, marked by bold chiaroscuro contrasts and by rich, intense colours, which were the result of the influence on the Neapolitan artist by Mattia Preti. Amongst the very finest examples of this period of Solimena's career is the canvas «Rebecca and Eleazar», painted around 1710, together with «Jacob and Rachel», for the Baglioni family of Rio Marin, Venice. A light which seems to be like a sudden flash of lightning makes the figures stand out with plastic presence. The compositional arrangement is a triangle, already typically eighteenth century in the elegant balancing of the links between the figures.

◀ **ALESSANDRO MAGNASCO** (1667-1749), *Christ adored by two nuns.* Oil on canvas (0,58×0,43) – c. 1715.

Alessandro Magnasco's first training was in the artistic circles of late seventeenth century Genoa where the styles most favourably regarded were those of Rubens and the painters of Lombardy with their considerable use of chiaroscuro, (Morazzone in particular). These influences led Magnasco towards a visionary, fantastic language characterized by stylistic modes of an expressionistic rapidity of execution and a tormented luministic violence. The pictoricism of Magnasco, of which «Christ adored by two nuns» is a significant example, worked on the imagination of many Venetian painters, and of Sebastiano and Marco Ricci and Francesco Guardi in particular.

SEBASTIANO RICCI (1660-1734), *Dream of Aesculapius.* Oil on canvas (0,62×1,01) – c. 1710.

After a long period of study of the greatest figures of late seventeenth century Italian painting, from Pietro da Cortona and Baciccio in Rome to the Carracci in Bologna, Luca Giordano in Florence and Magnasco in Milan, Sebastiano Ricci achieved a voice of his own characterized by a sparklingly fluent Rococo brilliance which was to gain the artist acceptance in London (1712-1716), and Paris (1716). Especially in paintings of small dimensions Sebastiano Ricci freed himself from all trace of his complex artistic training. Thus in the «Dream of Aesculapius» every detail of the bed chamber is rendered in the dancing rhythm of his line and the free and easy pictorial style. In the subdued glow of the setting, the scene seems like an animated ballet, fixed for ever in the wonder of bright, spirited colour.

◀ **GIOVANNI ANTONIO PELLEGRINI** (1675-1741), *Allegory of Sculpture*. Oil on canvas (1,42×1,32) – c. 1730; *Allegory of Painting*. Oil on canvas (1,43×1,32) – c. 1730.

Very early in his career, Giovanni Antonio Pellegrini, considerably influenced by Luca Giordano, absorbed the examples of Magnasco and Sebastiano Ricci and turned his style towards a refined decorative freedom in airily elegant works of pure rococo taste; and through his stays in several European artistic centres, London, Düsseldorf, The Hague, Antwerp, Paris, Prague, Dresden and Vienna, his work gained a certain popularity. The «Allegory of Sculpture» and the «Allegory of Painting» belong to his last years. They are an interweaving of the lightest of figural rhythms, a coloured web of impalpable, rarified weightlessness, shot through with silvery transparencies which recall the pastels of the artist's sister-in-law, Rosalba Carriera (cf. p. 90). Like hers, the paintings of Pellegrini are emblematic of the skin-deep spiritual frivolity of a part of the eighteenth century.

JACOPO AMIGONI (1675-1752), *Venus and Adonis*. Oil on canvas (0,45×0,75) – c. 1740.

Born in Naples but trained as an artist in Venice, Jacopo Amigoni soon began working in the Rococo style. Like Sebastiano Ricci and Pellegrino he often left Venice to work as one of Europe's foremost cosmopolitan artists, fixing the evanescent rather fragile delicacy of his style in great frescoes and paintings of historical subjects both profane and sacred. Charmingly Rococo in taste are the small canvases too, usually with some mythological or courtly subject. A typical example of this type is the painting of «Venus and Adonis», executed with arcadian grace in the sharpness of the composition and the clarity and softness of the colours soaked in a jewelled and diaphanous luminosity.

GIAMBATTISTA PITTONI (1687-1767), *Annunciation*. Oil on canvas (1,53×2,06) – 1758.

Of the many painters who followed Sebastiano Ricci and Pellegrini, very few achieved results of any degree of originality. Of those who did, Giambattista Pittoni turned the lessons of Ricci to his own use in a personal style whose elegant, rhythmic composition and delicate tonal clarity clearly announce his involvement in the world of rococo. Pittoni's taste for virtuoso display intensified still further towards the end of his career. It was in this period (1758) that he painted the «Annunciation» to decorate the «stanza dello studio» of the Old Academy which had been founded in 1750 at the Fonteghetto della Farina. The theatrical layout of the composition and the precious refinement of the drawing lend the sacred subject the air of an animated ballet with wonderfully fresh chromatic harmonies.

GIAMBATTISTA PIAZZETTA (1682-1754), *The Soothsayer*. Oil on canvas (1,54×1,14) – 1740.

In contrast with Sebastiano Ricci, Pellegrini and Amigoni, Giovanni Battista Piazzetta, after a period of study in Bologna in the «bottega» of Giuseppe Maria Crespi, settled in Venice permanently and developed his art and his career without leaving the city. At the beginning, his paintings were characterized by a harshly intense play of chiaroscuro and densely laid on paint, clearly the result of his contact with the robust brilliance of Crespi. Around half-way through the fourth decade of the eighteenth century, his painting relaxes somewhat into a style which is characterized by the sensually sonorous timbre of colour which he achieved by means of a light which his contemporaries called «lume solivo». The artist's masterpiece in this phase of his activity was «The Soothsayer» the real subject of which is the meeting of two young peasant-girls with one of them trying to attract the attention of the little dog which her companion is rather nonchalantly holding in her left arm. This moment of everyday life is transformed into pastoral idyll by the extremely careful fitting together of the planes of the scene and the grouping of the figures who are dominated by the glowing beauty of the young country-girl on whom the «lume solivo» concentrates and who thus becomes the highest note of the rich symphony of chromatic shadings.

GIULIA LAMA (1681-1747), *Judith and Holofernes*. Oil on canvas (1,07×1,55) – c. 1730.

Of the pupils of Piazzetta, Giulia Lama was certainly the one who showed the finest artistic temperament. She took her teacher's early period severity of colour and chiaroscuro and accentuated them in interpretations of vibrantly dramatic quality. In «Judith and Holofernes» the moment preceding the bloody event is charged with expressionistic accents through the violent effect with which the sudden aggressive light evokes the supine body of Holofernes, the figure of Judith intent in propitiary prayer and the figure of the old serving woman almost wholly enveloped in shadows. Such calculated and skilful scenic arrangement as seen in the foreshortening of the figures and the masterly control over the light, create an effect which is definitely not naturalistic but which aims rather at pleasing melodramatic intensity.

GIAMBATTISTA TIEPOLO (1696-1770), *The Rape of Europa*. Oil on canvas (0,99×1,34) – c. 1725; *Apollo and Marcia*. Oil on canvas (0,99×1,33) – c. 1725.

Giambattista Tiepolo very early withdrew from the lessons he was receiving from Gregorio Lazzarini, an academic of mediocre talents, and developed rather towards the vigorous chiaroscuro of Federico Bencovich and Piazzetta, rendering their solutions still more refined and precious by using colours which have an absolutely unmistakable, densely fused luminous vibration to them. At the end of this fundamental experience come the canvas of «The Rape of Europa» and «Apollo and Marcia» in which the mythological subjects are depicted in an airy, disenchanted transcription which at times becomes almost caricature. The severity of the pattern of chiaroscuro loses intensity in favour of refinement of chromatic notes in an interpretation of space open and articulated in depth which is as far from Bencovich and Piazzetta as it is consonant with the taste of Sebastiano Ricci. And the very lively spacial and luministic framework in which the figures take their places with such easy confidence offers a foretaste of the supreme gifts of Tiepolo as an «organizer» of paintings (cf. p. 65).

GIAMBATTISTA TIEPOLO, *The Holy House Transported from Nazareth to Loreto*. Oil on canvas (1,24×0,85) – c. 1742.

This preliminary sketch is one of the first for the now lost ceiling of the church of the Scalzi (cf. p. 87). Despite its limited dimensions the sketch gives a good idea of the spectacular grandeur and the virtuoso trompe l'oeil qualities of the fresco. It is clear too how even in the small canvases in which Tiepolo worked out his first thoughts the painter immediately went to the heart of the poetic inspiration of his subject and identified the chromatic values he was to adopt. Here he evokes the Holy Family with incomparable strength as they are borne on and preceded by flights of angels and as if drawn into the vastness of the celestial Empyrean where the Holy Trinity appears. Gestures and poses intertwine and disperse in musical phrases of infinite fluidity within the dream-like brightness and free symphony of brilliant, limpid colours.

GIANDOMENICO TIEPOLO (1727-1804), *Abraham and the Angels.* Oil on canvas (1,99×2,81) – 1773.

Giandomenico Tiepolo's early training was undertaken entirely in the ambit of his father Giambattista's art and the relationship was soon transformed into one of an anonymous collaborator, particularly on the great fresco projects. In his paintings of contemporary life and customs he tends to interpret reality carefully, often with ironic or grotesque overtones, while in his religious works Giandomenico clearly attempted to follow his father's example without however managing to achieve the easy flow of his line and his glorious colour. A characteristic example of his work is «Abraham and the Angels» which he painted in 1773 for the «New Chancellery» chamber of the Scuola di Santa Maria della Carità after his return from the Court in Madrid where he had gone with his father and brother Lorenzo in 1762. The static composure of the scene and the chalkiness of the colouring betray Giandomenico's meditations on the works of Mengs, the standard-bearer of neo-classical reform; at the same time it is clear that the artist's interest centres on the still life arrangement on the table which has been abandoned by Abraham as he hastens to prostrate himself before the three divine messengers.

VITTORE GHISLANDI (1655-1743), *Portrait of Count Giovanni Battista Vailetti.* Oil on canvas (2,26×1,37) – c. 1710.

The Bergamasque artist Vittore Ghislandi underwent a long apprenticeship in his two stays in Venice between 1675 and 1701, and combined the training received in Venice from the Baroque artist Sebastiano Bombelli and in Milan from Salomon Adler, still strongly influenced by Rembrandt, in a style of clearly realistic intentions, consonant with the great tradition of Lombard painting. Ghislandi exercised this predilection with incomparable strength in his portraits, of which the one depicting Count Giovanni Battista Vailetti is an excellent example. The nobleman's proud good looks and his serene control over his feelings are rendered with exceptional vividness as he poses in the intimacy of his study. There is a definite Enlightenment flavour in the realistic rendering of appearances in the portrait and in the acute psychological analysis it embodies.

ROSALBA CARRIERA (1675-1758), *Elderly Lady*. Pastel on paper (0,50×0,40) – c. 1740; *Cardinal Melchior de Polignac*. Pastel on paper (0,57×0,46) – c. 1732; *Young Cavalier*. Pastel on paper (0,55×0,42) c. 1730; *Young lady of the Leblond family*. Pastel on paper (0,34×0,27) – c. 1730.

A sister-in-law of G. A. Pellegrini (cf. p. 83), Rosalba Carriera achieves the same airy lightness of touch as her relative in her portraits. These were done in pastel and in them she explored the finest shadings of her subjects' characters, the most fleeting of their moods. Thus, without falling either into the dangers of the encomiastic portrait or of the documentary, Rosalba matches the immediacy of pastel technique to the freshness of her psychological and social penetration of her subjects, offering an unrivalled picture of the society of her time. In the «Elderly Lady» the mature beauty of the noblewoman and her serene, good-natured existence are conveyed with incomparable skill. No less typical of her work is the portrait of Cardinal Melchior de Polignac with its superb rendering of the physical features of the subject, catching immediately the wilful character of the prelate. Likewise, the artist uses her pastels with consummate skill in conveying the vanity of the «Young Cavalier» and the fresh innocence of the «Young Lady of the Leblond Family».

PIETRO LONGHI (1702-1785), *The Concert*. Oil on canvas (0,60×0,48) – 1741; *The Venetian Lady's Morning*. Oil on canvas (0,60×0,49) – c. 1741; *The Spice-vendor's shop* (0,60×0,48) c. 1752; *The Soothsayer* (0,60×0,49) – c. 1750.

After several unfortunate attempts at historical paintings, Pietro Falca, known as Pietro Longhi, turned, on his return from a stay in Bologna where he had particularly admired the popular art of Giuseppe Maria Crespi, to the depicting of Venetian society at the moment of its decline, offering a witty view, with just a hint of irony, in which not even the smallest detail that can lend colour is neglected. Though the paintings look similar, they in fact offer an extremely wide range of subtly described and individualized personalities and moods of the characters engaged in often frivolous pursuits under the gaze, alternately ironic and ambiguous, of servants who rarely betray any sympathy or liking for their masters and mistresses. In the minute detail of his sharp reporting Pietro Longhi sees his age with a spirit of good-humoured optimism untinged by social and moral judgements. His art shows a close affinity with the work of Carlo Goldoni, a connection that was several times acknowledged by the great playwright himself.

ALESSANDRO LONGHI (1733-1813), *Portrait of the Pisani family*. Oil on canvas (2,55×3,41) – c. 1758.

A pupil of his father, Pietro, and like him not very gifted in the field of historical and sacred paintings, Alessandro Longhi devoted himself to portraiture transposing the figures which populate his father's paintings into life-size portraits, maintaining at the same time the impassive line and colourful palette of the older painter. Thus, in his vast early portrait of the Pisani family, Alessandro Longhi seems at once to be imitating the pungently expressive efficiency of his father and at the same time to be transposing it into a decoratively pompous style which anticipates the grotesques of Goya without, however, the latter's satirical overtones.

ALESSANDRO LONGHI, *Portrait of Father Carlo Lodoli*. Oil on canvas (1,30×0,95) – c. 1765.

Occasionally Alessandro Longhi achieves high points of immediacy of presentation and psychological insight by means of the essentially sober quality of the range of colours used. This is the style chosen to present the moral gravity of Father Carlo Lodoli, the famous Venetian architectural theoretician and censor of architects. The features of his face are faithfully traced, his bushy eyebrows, the brilliant eyes, the large nose and the firm, straight set of the mouth.

GASPARE TRAVERSI (1732-1769), *The Wounded Man*. Oil on canvas (1,01×1,27) – c. 1752.

At the same time as Traversi was painting the Neapolitan artist Gaspare Traversi also dedicated himself to scenes of family life and customs which were still more openly realistic than those of the Venetian. Of these «The Wounded Man» is rightly considered to be one of the finest examples. Unmoved, the light defines the physical features and emotions of the participants in the scene: the pain of the young man who, supported by the weeping girl, raises his shirt so that the doctor can examine his wound; the cold professional detachment of the doctor; the helplessness of the assistant who, with the grief-stricken parents, is convinced of the uselessness of any treatment. In the «tranche de vie» crudely caught between light and shade the lesson of Caravaggio falls back into a realism reminiscent of the rational spirit of the Enlightenment.

ANTONIO CANAL known as **CANALETTO** (1697-1768), *Perspective*. Oil on canvas (1,31×0,93) – 1765.

If the attention of Rosalba Carriera and Pietro Longhi was drawn to the life and customs of their own day, Canaletto left for posterity a panorama of the colourfully spectacular public life of Venice, all registered in his precisely drawn and perspectively accurate scenes. He soon turned his back on the confident virtuoso displays of scenery painting and designing which he had been given a start in by his father Bernardo. And after a period in Rome where he was struck more by the objective reporting of reality by Viviano Coduzzi and painters from the Netherlands like Berkheide than the decorative vivacity of Pannini and Van Wittel, Canaletto applied himself to setting onto canvas scenes from Venice as later he was to paint views of London and the English countryside. In these paintings he conceded nothing to the episodic and the picturesque and concentrated his clear-sighted vision instead on creating a space-light synthesis of extraordinary truthfulness. The «Perspective», Canaletto's entry for admission to the Accademia in September, 1763 is a fine example of his extraordinary recreation of real data in prodigiously stylized form. Even though here the subject is drawn from the imagination, each architectural detail is a fascinating concentration of images.

BERNARDO BELLOTTO (1720-1780), *The Scuola of San Marco*. Oil on canvas (0,42×0,69) – 1738-40.

A nephew and follower of Canaletto, Bernardo Bellotto applies the clear reporter's vision of the master to a slower and more intimate exploration of reality. And from his earliest works, Bellotto softens the formal rigour of Canaletto into natural, simple, concrete observations, and his brilliant, kaleidoscopic palette into a dense range of colours, tending towards the coldly bright. In the «Rio dei Mendicanti» the buildings of the left bank lie partly in shadow and partly in full sunlight. And beyond the bridge standing between light and shade, the dome of the Emiliani chapel in the church of S. Michele in Isola can be seen in the distance. On the opposite bank the corners of the Scuola of San Marco and the seventeenth century building in the foreground are darkened as the shadows of the hour before sunset gather. The density of the chiaroscuro and the paint itself lend the view a fascinating concreteness with every detail assuming an undramatized presence.

MICHELE MARIESCHI (1710-1743), *Imaginative view with obelisk*. Oil on canvas (0,55×0,82) – c. 1735. ➧

Unlike the views of Canaletto, those of Michele Marieschi clearly betray signs of their creator's youthful activity as a stage-designer. His decorative paintings seem to combine the tender freshness of the colours of Zuccarelli and the witty, rapid brush-work of Marco Ricci. This is the background to the «Imaginative view with obelisk», its perspective layout scenographically grandiose and its drawing delicate and colourful, its architecture and foreground groups brilliant and sharp, the landscape background diaphanously soft, almost transparent on the horizon of the lagoon beyond the ferry gondola.

FRANCESCO GUARDI (1712-1793), *The Island of S. Giorgio Maggiore.* Oil on canvas (0,72×0,97) – c. 1780.

Developing the palette of Magnasco and the lighter version of Sebastiano and Marco Ricci, Francesco Guardi offers an interpretation of eighteenth century Venice which is diametrically opposed to that of Canaletto. Instead of Canaletto's lucid and truthful objectivity of space and perspective, Francesco Guardi offered a romantic vision in which appearances of reality are evoked in ephemeral suggestions of colour. In this magical optical illusion the spell cast by Venice leaps to the surface and fixes itself in the memory for ever. A good example of this transfiguration which remains at the same time so faithful to reality is the «View of the Island of S. Giorgio», one of several treatments of the same scene. Against the azure sky streaked with pink and the shadowed greens of the lagoon, architecture, people, and objects acquire a magical lightness. And in the ever-changing scenario of water, sky and stone this much-loved Venetian landmark, the island of San Giorgio and the shadowed tip of the Giudecca take form in a new, extraordinary, magically allusive image.

FRANCESCO GUARDI, *Blaze in the oil warehouses at S. Marcuola*. Oil on canvas (0,41×0,60) – 1789.

Francesco Guardi's incomparable ability to recreate reality was no less potent when he was commissioned to produce commemorative paintings on the occasion of visits by illustrious personages or of important events. One of these works is the «Blaze in the oil warehouses at S. Marcuola» which broke out on the evening of 28th. December, 1789. In the apocalyptic fire the swirling smoke which blacks out the sky is shot through with flashes of reflections from the flames and in their light onlookers stand edging the bank of the canal to watch the event, to comment on the progress of the fire and to follow the efforts of those busy pouring buckets of water on the roofs and removing burnt articles. All the tragic desolation of the event is evoked in exemplary fashion with a sober palette and a touch which is precise despite the very small dimensions of the painting.

ROOM 20

(of the stories of the Cross)

The most important commissioners of artistic works in Venice were the Scuole, those characteristic institutions formed of persons belonging to one of the professions or national groupings who gathered together as confraternities which functioned as charities. The imposing series of pictures (known as «teleri») painted for the Scuole around the end of the fifteenth century hold a particular interest and importance because of the evidence they contain about the life and customs in the Venice of the time. From this point of view, amongst the most representative of these cycles of «teleri» is the one painted for the Scuola Grande di San Giovanni Evangelista by the most famous «pittori di ceremonia» or ceremonial artists of the day: Gentile Bellini, Vittore Carpaccio, Benedetto Diana, Giovanni Mansueti and Lorenzo Bastiani. The eight canvases decorated the room in the Scuola where the relic of the Holy Cross was kept, having been donated to the Confraternity in

1369 by Philippe de Mézières, Grand Chancellor of the Kingdom of Cyprus. The cycle now in the collection of the Galleries was itself probably a substitute for an earlier cycle, commissioned by the members of the Confraternity as far back as 1414 following a miracle which happened that year as a result of prayers to the relic.

GENTILE BELLINI (1429-1507), *Procession in St. Mark's Square*. Tempera and oil on canvas (3,67×7,45) – 1496.

For the Scuola of San Giovanni Evangelista Gentile Bellini painted three «teleri». The first is dated 1496 and represents the miraculous intervention of the Holy Cross in St. Mark's Square on 25th. April, 1444 on the occasion of the Feast of the Holy Cross. During the procession a merchant from Brescia by the name of Jacopo de' Salis knelt before the relic of the Holy Cross being carried by the members of the Confraternity of San Giovanni Evangelista and prayed that his dying son should be saved. The son recovered immediately. In the incomparable wideangle view the spectacle of St. Mark's Square and the ceremony taking place unfold. On the left, the Procuratie Vecchie are still the one-storey buildings there since the time of Doge Sebastiano Ziani (1172-1178); the Gothic buildings which lie beyond were demolished in the early sixteenth century to make way for the construction of the Clock Tower designed by Coducci. At the end of the square the Basilica of St. Mark still glows with the gold of the marble decorations and the Veneto-Byzantine mosaics of which the only one that survives is the one above the arched doorway on the left. The Porta della Carta too stands splendid in its original gilded marble decorations, a brilliant caesura between the Basilica and the Palace of the Doges. On the right, grouped around the base of the campanile stands the cluster of buildings including the Orseolo Hospice which was to be demolished in the sixteenth century so that the Procuratie Nuove could be built in its place as part of the plan for the Square produced by Jacopo Sansovino. The ancient buildings reflect the reddish bricks of the floor of the square which remained until Tirali changed them for the present grey slabs of stone patterned with white marble in 1723. The painter's attention was no less committed when reporting the procession. While the members of the government with the Doge at their head preceded by the standard-bearers, the trumpeters and the symbols of power, are level with the campanile, the members of the Confraternity stand out in the foreground, dressed in the white habits of the Scuola. In the middle of the group escorted by candle-bearers and torch-bearers a canopy covers a golden «soler» on which is carried the precious relic of the Holy Cross. Reality in the scene is treated faithfully and in minute detail and to encompass the whole event the perspective is widened artificially. In this «mediaeval» canvas Gentile Bellini achieves a choral grandeur within which be fixes his portrait of men and buildings.

GENTILE BELLINI, *The Miracle of the Cross recovered from the canal of S. Lorenzo.* Tempera on canvas (3,23×4,30) – a. 1500.

Dated 1500, this is the second of the «teleri» painted by Gentile Bellini for the Holy Cross cycle at the Scuola of San Giovanni Evangelista. According to legend the miraculous event took place between 1370 and 1382 during the annual procession when the relic of the Holy Cross was carried from the Scuola to the church of S. Lorenzo. When the procession was crossing the bridge in front of the church of S. Lorenzo the relic was pushed into the waters of the canal by the crowd. The relic floated, miraculously eluding the grasp of all the faithful who dived into the canal to save it; all except Andrea Vendramin, the Grand Guardian of the Scuola. The scene is registered with documentary fidelity but is seen as though through a watery light. The same rarified atmosphere overlays both participant in the event and the spectators of the miracle who include real contemporary figures: Caterina Cornaro, Queen of Cyprus, is the first of the ladies kneeling on the stage on the left, and in the group of gentlemen on the right Gentile included portraits of himself and his brother Giovanni. Incomparable fifteenth century Venice then, with its buildings decorated with highly coloured frescos and painted plaster work, with its round chimney-pots and equally characteristic jutting grills, provides a colourful and poetically archaic setting for the event. And the many characters who people the picture seem to be participants in a scene of enchantment, inhabiting a magically still atmosphere, figures set in relief against the deep green of the waters of the canal frozen forever in this moment of time.

GENTILE BELLINI, *The Healing of Pietro dei Ludovici.* Tempera on canvas (3,69×2,59) – a. 1501 c.

Probably completed in 1501, this canvas depicts the healing of Pietro dei Ludovici, afflicted with ague. The miracle, which occurred through contact with a processional candle which had touched the relic of the Holy Cross, takes place inside a chapel which is in large part occupied by an extremely elegant ciborium surmounted by the eagle symbol of St. John the Evangelist. This detail and also the triptych on the altar which recalls the one painted by Bastiani in his canvas depicting the «Donation ot the Relic», suggests that Gentile Bellini wished here to set the scene in the interior of the church of St. John the Evangelist. Echoing his father Jacopo's interest in Renaissance «umbratile» as shown in his book of drawings now in the British Museum in London, Gentile Bellini concentrates on the detailed rendering of the complex play of architectural surfaces within which his human figures play their part.

VITTORE CARPACCIO (1465 c.-1523/26), *The Healing of the Madman*. Tempera on canvas (3,65×3,89) – a. 1496 c.

The subject of this «telero» is the healing of a man possessed performed by Francesco Querini, the Patriarch of Grado, through the intercession of the relic of the Holy Cross in his palace at the Rialto. The actual miracle is relegated to a position in the upper left part of the picture and takes place in the wonderfully airy loggia of the palace. This allows attention to be centred on the view of Rialto Bridge and the banks on either side of the Grand Canal. The bridge depicted is the one built in 1458; at its sides can be seen the shops and in the centre the part which could be raised to allow the taller ships to pass. This construction, which was of wood, collapsed on 4th. August, 1524 and was replaced by the present stone bridge which was opened in 1592. On the left bank, amid the ancient structures can be seen the sign of the Storione Hotel, which stood in a side road, while in the background, behind the bridge, the «loggia» of the Rialto can be made out, a much-used meeting-place for users of the market. On the right bank are visible the Fondaco dei Tedeschi, destroyed by fire in 1505, Ca' da Mosto with its open canal-side entrance which still exists, and the old campanile of the church of Santi Apostoli which was reconstructed in 1672. All the descriptive precision of the physical surroundings does

not cause the work to degenerate into the merely documentary, but acts as a lively support to the scene. On the black waters of the Grand Canal and along its banks the intense daily life of the place runs its course while the noble men and the very elegant «compagni della Calza» cluster around below the loggia of the Palace of the Patriarch of Grado and the buildings with their round chimney-pots stand out against the pale blue and pink sky. Each manifestation of reality is caught in its truest aspect, its most accurate shade of colour, in this evocation of a relaxed and airy fifteenth century Venice, a representation which is a long way from the «inventory» style adopted by the other contemporary «ceremonial» painters.

LAZZARO BASTIANI (1429-1514), *The Relic of the Holy Cross is offered to the Scuola di S. Giovanni Evangelista*. Tempera on canvas (3,19×4,38) – a. 1494 c.

This canvas depicts the most important moment in the history of the relic of the Holy Cross: the ceremony at which it was offered to the Scuola di S. Giovanni Evangelista by Philippe de Mézières in 1369. The event, which takes place inside the church of S. Giovanni Evangelista, is seen from outside and documents the appearence, today completely changed, of one of the most typical architectural features of Venice: the brick building, fronted by a portico decorated with frescos and surmounted by a terrace with a richly ornamented surrounding balustrade, which contained the cemetery. Inside the church the polygonal apse can be glimpsed, together with tall, narrow windows and on the altar a polyptych which is very reminiscent of the one included by Gentile Bellini in his painting of the «Miraculous Healing of Pietro de' Ludovici». In this «telero» Lazzaro Bastiani was evidently attempting to emulate the choral grandeur achieved by Gentile Bellini and the fascinating evocation of Vittore Carpaccio. But his interpretation of the Venice of the time remains little more than prosaic and rather suggests an analytical report. The interest of the painting therefore lies principally in its value as an irreplaceable historical document offering evidence of an urban Venice which has now disappeared for ever.

GIOVANNI MANSUETI, *The Miraculous Healing of the daughter of Benvegnudo of S. Polo.* Tempera on canvas (3,69×2,96) – a. 1505 c.

The subject of this «telero» is the miraculous healing in 1414 of the little daughter of Benvegnudo. Having been paralysed ever since birth, she gained the use of her limbs after touching the three candles which her father had placed on the relic of the Holy Cross. The interior of the richly decorated and furnished room and the animation of the watching crowd are described with inventorial precision.

GIOVANNI MANSUETI (known 1485-1527), *Miracle of the Relic of the Holy Cross in Campo S. Lio.* Tempera on canvas (3,18×4,58) – a. 1494.

This canvas deals with a miraculous event which took place in 1474 during the funeral of a member of the Confraternity who had not believed firmly in the relic of the Holy Cross during his life. The reliquary containing the sacred fragment was taken to the funeral in the church of S. Lio but in the square outside the church it became so heavy that it could not be carried over the threshold. Another cross had therefore to be used while the one containing the Holy relic was entrusted to the care of the parish priest of S. Lio. The presentation of Campo S. Lio is rather static and analytical, the figural rhythms monotonous and the colouring somewhat lacking in richness and interest, but the picture is nevertheless valuable for the evidence it offers of the architecture and costumes of the time.

BENEDETTO DIANA (known 1482-1525), *Miracle of the relic of the Holy Cross.* Tempera on canvas (3,65×1,47) – a. 1505-1510.

Having passed from the influence of Bastiani and Antonello da Messina to a meditation on the works of Gentile Bellini and Vittore Carpaccio, Benedetto Diana was able, at the beginning of the sixteenth century, to absorb the influences of the most modern of painters working in Venice, of Lotto and Giorgione in particular. He showed a constant, natural predisposition for large-scale monumental compositions however and for the precise spacial geometry of late fifteenth century tradition. This inclination is also clearly displayed in the «telero» painted for the Hostel Chamber of the Scuola di San Giovanni Evangelista. According to the «Descrizione» of the Scuola published in 1787, the painting tells the story of how the four-year-old son of Alvise Finetti, «scrivan alla Camera degli imprestidi» recovered after sustaining mortal injuries in a fall from the loft of his house. Especially evocative is the description of the interior courtyard of a fifteenth century Venetian palace reminiscent in its freely atmospheric style of Carpaccio.

ROOM 21

(of the Story of St. Ursula)

In 1306, six years after the establishment of the Confraternity of St. Ursula, a headquarters for the order was built at the side of the right apse of the church of SS. Giovanni e Paolo. It was only in 1488 however that a decision was reached that the oratory should be decorated with paintings telling the story of St. Ursula. Vittore Carpaccio was commissioned to do the work. After the first «telero» of 1490, «The Arrival in Cologne», the other seven paintings followed not in the order of their subject matter but rather as space on the walls was made ready. Vittore Carpaccio drew his inspiration for the cycle from the «Lives of the Saints» by Jacopo da Varazze, published in Venice in an Italian translation by Nicolò Minerbi in 1475. But Carpaccio changed the emphasis of the story from the sacred to the profane and achieved a vivid representation of the life and customs of the time within a framework of settings reminiscent of the Venetian lagoon and mainland in which figure prominently monumental buildings typical of those created for the reconstruction of Venice undertaken around the end of the fifteenth century by the Lombardos and Coducci.

VITTORE CARPACCIO (1465 c. – 1526), *The Arrival of the English Ambassadors at the Court of Brittany*. Tempera on canvas (2,75×5,89) – 1495-1500.

This «telero», though it depicts the first of the episodes of the story, was amongst the last to be painted. In it the ambassadors of the pagan King of England are seen arriving at the court of the King of Brittany with the proposal that the son of the English King should marry Ursula, the daughter of the Christian king. On the right, Ursula lays down to her father the conditions on which she will accept the proposal: that the groom shall be baptized and that the couple shall undertake a long pilgrimage accompanied by ten thousand virgins. The warm light of mid-day bathes the scene from the left and highlights every detail of the rich composition in a secure grid of colour and sharply outlined shadows. The architecture is reminiscent of the ideas of Coducci and the Lombardo family; the highly decorated column of variegated marble and glinting metals sharply redolent of the world of Ferrara; the ambassadors kneeling deferentially in an act of homage, quite apart from one another as demanded by protocol; the king and his ministers ranged in dignified expectation against the wall; the spectators of the event, some of them curious, others, like the four elegant young men on the left, quite indifferent. Also participants in the enchanted spectacle are the small figures whose shadows fall across the sun-bathed bank beyond which stretches the spacious outline of a lagoon city. Though it is cast from two distinct sources, the light on the right is no less strongly evocative as it illuminates Ursula talking in her room with her father. The fluid vibrations of the half-light give rise to an atmosphere of domestic intimacy which also embraces the old servant woman huddled at the foot of the staircase only too filled with foreboding about the tragic epilogue which the royal marriage contract is to have.

VITTORE CARPACCIO, *The English Ambassadors take their leave.* Tempera on canvas (2,18×2,53) – 1495-1500.

This «telero» was probably the last to be painted by Carpaccio. In it, the light is not used to draw attention to the calm intimacy of Ursula's chamber but rather highlights the cold elegance of officialdom; the English ambassadors take their leave of the King of Brittany while the court scribe takes down the dictated reply to the King of England containing the marriage terms. The closely interwoven foreshortenings in the perspective arrangement of the chamber are organized in impeccable purity of form, as are the principal and secondary characters participating in the event, each of them caught in the garments and gestures which most clearly allude to their various ranks and offices, and this purity extends beyond the door thrown open to reveal the complex staircase which climbs past the grandiose heavily shadowed archway, and the city glimpsed in the distance through the sharp clarity of the air.

VITTORE CARPACCIO, *The English Ambassadors return home*. Tempera on canvas (2,95×5,27) – 1495-1500.

This canvas, like the two previous ones, can be dated to the very last years of the fifteenth century. Its setting is a port, dominated on the right by a grand Renaissance palace which stands almost as a symbol of the architecturally designed paintings of Carpaccio. The whole composition is organized around the diagonals which define the perspective of the palace which competes with the contemporary buildings of Coducci: the bridge and the canal bank heaving with people, the royal pavilion, the buildings lining the canal which winds lazily around the towers. The rich, dense colour contributes to the magic spell cast by the light as it falls on planes strictly controlled by the scheme of perspective. In the diffused afternoon light the colours dissolve into warm tonalities which lend a sumptuousness to the silken robes, the elegant head-dresses and even the brick and marble facings of the buildings. Testifying to the fact that the spectacle we are witnessing is that of late fifteenth century Venice are not only the colourful buildings but also several precise details: the ambassador walking majestically on the left of the scene closely resembles a «Compagno della Calza» in full ceremonial dress and the «Scalco» (the official who, preceded by musicians, announced the arrival of ambassadors and showed them into the apartments of the Doge) is seated beneath the banner which flutters high up in the sea breeze. In this presentation of a Venice which is not actually topographically identifiable but which appears transformed by the power of imagination in its unique atmosphere, impervious to the passing of time, Vittore Carpaccio expresses his singular humanistic vision of the world.

VITTORE CARPACCIO, *Ursula meets Ereus and the Piligrims Depart.* Tempera on canvas (2,80×6,11) – 1495.

This «telero», signed by Carpaccio and dated 1495, depicts four significant moments of the legend: on the left Ereus takes leave of his father; on the right, beyond the banner, the bride and groom meet and immediately afterwards say farewell to Ursula's parents; also on the right in the background, Ursula and Ereus board the sloop to reach the large ship which is ready, with sails unfurled, to set off. The episodes succeed each other in an uninterrupted sequence of absolute clarity, the artist organizing the broad canvas in such a way as to maintain at the same time the unity of the whole. And every detail of the scene takes its place in the overall architectural unity of the piece positioned not casually as might at first appear but skilfully subordinated to the dictates of the light. On the left the English city is defended by several impregnable castles of perfectly regular geometrical dimensions. As the human figures turn, their richly coloured garments glow sumptuously in the reflected light. In the landscape several details taken from identifiable geographical

locations can be identified such as the two towers of Rhodes and Candia reflected in the greenish waters of the lagoon; behind these towers rises a hill which is much more reminiscent of the view at Marostica than Corfù from which it is supposed to be derived. To match this magical evocation of the Veneto mainland the right hand section of the picture offers the no less intense view of Venice itself rising undefended straight out of the waters of the lagoon. The pure architectural language of the buildings and their highly coloured marble facades suggest a fascinating transposition in pictorial terms of the motifs of buildings planned and constructed along the banks of the Grand Canal and all over Venice by the architects of the Lombardo family and Coducci. Another immediate reminder of Venice in holiday mood is the sight of people crowding into balconies, staircases, bridges, along the banks of the canals and in the boats which rock gently in the glassy waters of the lagoon. Then there are the luxurious costumes and the oriental carpets laid out in the sun. The whole amazing scene is like a brilliant kaleidoscope in which every detail is picked out with eye-catching, colourful precision and set down with impassive detatchment, and it has no equal amongst other paintings «di ceremonia» in the Venice of the day.

VITTORE CARPACCIO, *Dream of St. Ursula*. Tempera on canvas (2,74×2,67) – 1495.

In her chamber, Ursula receives the announcement of her coming martyrdom brought to her in her sleep by an angel. The warm room, its furniture and furnishings described in every smallest detail, is only just lightened by the dawn. In the subtle pattern of light and shade all the ornaments in the room, like Ursula herself absorbed in her dream, seem to participate in a general atmosphere of expectancy before the sudden appearance of the angel bearing the palm of the martyr, whose arrival is heralded by the shadow clearly etched on the floor. In this «telero» more than in any of the others, the localized value of colour seems to determine the atmospheric sense in a way that foreshadows the tonal revolution of Giorgione (cf. p. 38).

VITTORE CARPACCIO, *The Pilgrims meet Pope Cyriac.* Tempera on canvas (2,81×3,07) c. 1492.

The meeting between Ursula and Ereus and Pope Cyriac takes place before the walls of Castel S. Angelo in Rome. In the brilliant mid-day light, while the procession of virgins is still making its way along the path from the landing-stage where the ships have cast anchor, the couple genuflect before the Pope who has come out to meet them accompanied by bishops, prelates and other dignitaries. Though other of the «teleri» painted later may display greater fluency of composition, this canvas is nevertheless characterized by a skilful and sure organization of «geometrical» surfaces in relation to the light whether they be the severe architectural shapes of Castel S. Angelo or the crowds of brilliantly colourful human figures who are disposed against the yellow-green of the open space like sparkling prisms in a spectacular setting which is even a little too carefully calculated, as happens too in the painting of the «Arrival in Cologne» of 1490.

VITTORE CARPACCIO, *The Arrival of the pilgrims in Cologne.* Tempera on canvas (2,80×2,55) – 1490.

The first to be painted of the cycle of pictures dedicated to the legend of St. Ursula is also the earliest known painting by Carpaccio. Two episodes are depicted: on the right, the Hunnish leaders read the message from a group of traitorous Roman princes warning them of the arrival of the Christian pilgrims; on the left, the ship bearing Ursula and Pope Cyriac is already riding at anchor in the harbour of Cologne. If on the one hand the attempt to impose a unity on the two separate episodes is rather forced, on the other the slow rhythm of the narration immediately succeeds in catching just the right fabled tone for the legend.

VITTORE CARPACCIO, *Martyrdom of the Pilgrims and the funeral of Ursula*. Tempera on canvas (2,72×5,60) – 1493.

The column which rises from the beautiful plinth decorated with the entwined arms of the Loredan and Caotorta families separates two episodes of the legend: on the left, the slaughter of Ursula, Pope Cyriac and their companions; on the right, the funeral of the saint. Whereas in the «Arrival in Cologne» and the «Meeting of the Pilgrims with Pope Cyriac» there was still uncertainty and hesitancy in the artist's organization of the canvas, here he has reached a confident maturity of style. Comparing this «telero» with the two painted previously one notices a definite change of direction in Carpaccio's style due to his absorption of many influences: the visual precision of the Flemish painters; the harmonies of the sublime world of Giovanni Bellini; the clear narrative force of the Ferrara artists based on the fortunate conjunction of Andrea Mantegna, Piero della Francesca and Rogier van der Weyden; the elegantly refined spacial innovations of the Umbrians, especially Perugino. The last moments of the life of Ursula fit fluently and neatly into the pattern of perspective adopted. The whole composition revolves around the warrior in the centre, in the act of unsheathing his

sword. Above him flutters the pink and white oriflamme which follows the line of the undulating countryside stretching away into the distance, a hilly Veneto mainland where warriors joust as in an ancient tournament. Participant too in this world of ecstatic silences is the fine bowman calmly taking aim at the kneeling Ursula, absorbed in prayer. Behind her the fury of the massacre is unleashed in a scene reminiscent of the fresco by Tommaso da Modena in the church of S. Margherita in Treviso and the slaughter is carried back into the infinite distance by the rapidly diminishing perspective of the line of trees. On the other side of the picture, likewise set amongst the gently rolling Veneto hills, the funeral of Ursula takes place. Human figures and architectural forms all participate in a perfect, colourful geometrical patterning highlighted by the bright, clear light. Despite his supreme concentration on the organization of his canvas, Carpaccio found space for several portraits of contemporaries including one of Eugenia Caotorta, the wife of Angelo Loredan who is pictured kneeling on the right in the clothes not of a nobleman but of a lay-priest, the garments in which he wished to be buried. In this canvas Carpaccio had clearly achieved the ability to organize and intensify everyday reality to the point where it becomes an abstraction of poetically allusive force. Proof of this arises clearly from consideration of the «The Departure of the Pilgrims» and the three «teleri» (cf. p. 106-111) involving the ambassadors.

VITTORE CARPACCIO, *Apotheosis of St. Ursula*. Tempera on canvas (4,81×3,36) – 1491.

Within the grandiose chapel, surrounded by cherubs, under the welcoming arms of the Eternal Father, Ursula rises gloriously beyond a band of palm leaves above all those who accompanied her on the fateful pilgrimage. And to the right, beside the Pope, Vittore Carpaccio painted three contemporaries, influential members of the Confraternity, who witness the apotheosis of the saint. Even more than in the dense pattern of the virgins' heads, and the superimposition of the saint, the cherubs and the Eternal Father, which is rather reminiscent of Mantegna, the poetry of Carpaccio is to be sensed in the landscape passage, richly suggestive of the Veneto countryside, which fills the background of the picture against the vibrant silvery brightness of the sky.

ROOM 23

(The church of S. Maria della Carità)

The church of S. Maria della Carità was built by the workshop of Bartolomeo Bon between 1441 and 1452. It was modelled on the church of San Gregorio, with a single nave and three polygonal apses; the roof was supported by open wooden beams. The «coronation of the Virgin» in the lunette above the entrance was carved between 1443 – 4 by Bartolomeo Bon. Over the centuries the interior of the church was embellished by numerous altars, magnificent sepulchral monuments to the Doge Da Ponte and to the Barbarigos, four triptychs by Giovanni Bellini and altar-pieces by Antonio Vivarini, Vittore Carpaccio, Giambattista Cima and Leandro Bassano. When, at the beginning of the 19th century, the Carità was chosen as the seat of the new Academy, the church was stripped of its works of art and divided to make two floors. The schools were housed on the ground floor and the Abbot Farsetti's collection of sculpture on the upper one. Today, this well lighted space has been made into two areas: one for exhibitions and teaching and the other reserved for Venetian painting of the second half of the 15th century, including the four triptychs by the young Giovanni Bellini which have been returned to their original home. The works in the collection are significant as an indication of the reactionary attitude of Venetian painters to the revolutionary new developments noted in Padua around the middle of the century in works by Donatello and Mantegna and in Venice in the presence of Antonello da Messina.

GENTILE BELLINI (1429-1507), *The blessed Lorenzo Giustiniani*. Tempera on canvas (2,21×1,55) – 1465.

Gentile Bellini, like his brother Giovanni, after a natural apprenticeship with his father Jacopo, was influenced by the new developments from Tuscany which had a flourishing centre in Padua led by Donatello. But from his early works onwards he tended towards an interpretation, still mediaeval in spirit, of the classicism of his brother-in-law, Andrea Mantegna. In this work portraying Lorenzo Giustiniani just nine years after his death (1456), which was originally in the church of Madonna dell'Orto, the search for three dimensional form is undermined by the evident design and the simplified spatial perspective. Gentile Bellini is an observer who here transcribes with harsh realism the physical features of a man worn out by age and asceticism.

GIOVANNI BELLINI (c. 1430-1516), *Nativity Triptych*. Tempera on wood (1,03×0,45 central panel; 1,27×0,48 side panels; 0,60×1,66 lunette) – 1462/64.

This is one of the four triptychs (in the church of S. Maria della Carità) which represent an important stage in the work of the youthful Giovanni Bellini. The influence of Mantegna and Donatello is evident in the four works painted for the Andrea Molin chapel, especially in the lunette. Here the figures stand out clearly on the gold ground, now devoid of all transcendental significance, respecting laws of perspective and symmetry as well as of tone and colour, bathing the central panel in light. The subject of the central panel recalls a work of 1447 by Vivarini, now in the Prague National Gallery.

GIOVANNI BELLINI, *St. Sebastian Triptych*. Tempera on wood (1,03×0,45 central panel; 1,27×0,48 side panels; 0,59×1,70 lunette) – 1460/64.

This triptych, the altar-piece of the chapel of St. Sebastiano (in the church of S. Maria della Carità), was commissioned by Zaccaria Vitturini. It also shows the influence of the vibrant energy of Donatello and the rigorous plasticity of Mantegna, made softer and more natural by Bellini's use of colour. In a few details, as in the face of St. Sebastian standing out clearly in its golden halo, one already senses the beginnings of the Christian spirituality which the 70 year-old Bellini was able to express in terms of a humanistic formal purity.

BARTOLOMEO VIVARINI (c. 1432-1491), *Conversano Polyptych*. Tempera on wood (1,57×2,71 total measurements) – 1475.

The works of Bartolomeo Vivarini, pupil first of his brother, Antonio (cf. p. 125) and then of Andrea Mantegna, can be compared with those of Cosmè Tura and Carlo Crivelli although they do not achieve the same high poetic quality. The influence of Renaissance ideas on his work is hampered by a tormented plasticity which is still Gothic, by strong contrasts of tone and a decorative line. The Conversano Polyptych, signed and dated 1475 is painted with the same unfailing constancy, the same archaic flavour that we find in all his brightly coloured altar-pieces. In the central Nativity scene the countryside appears to climb with a «Gothic steepness» up to the narrow sky devoid of any atmospheric effect.

BARTOLOMEO VIVARINI, *St. Ambrose Polyptych*. Tempera on wood (1,25×0,47, central panel; 1,08×0,36, side panels) – 1477.

Unlike Mantegna's humanistic ideals of beauty, the rigour of Bartolomeo Vivarini's tormented vision is not softened even by the influence of the lyricism of Giovanni Bellini. In the St. Ambrose polyptych Vivarini still uses the impenetrable gold ground on which the figures with their obvious sculptural quality, stand in isolation, each within their own compartment on their marble plinth of uncertain perspective. In the central panel the icon-like figure of St. Ambrose sits rigid on his throne, while at his feet the members of the stonecutters' guild kneel in the proportions dictated by the Mediaeval iconographic tradition.

ANDREA DA MURANO (active 1462-1502), *Polyptych*. Tempera on wood (1,52×0,88 central panel; 1,52×0,47 side panels; 0,80×1,99 lunette) – c. 1475.

Unlike Bartolomeo Vivarini, the early works of Andrea da Murano display the fullness of sculptural form and clarity of spatial structure which we note in the works of Giovanni Bellini. His masterpiece of this period is the polyptych, originally in the church of St. Peter Martyr of Murano. Although conceived according to the traditional dividing up into compartments, with St. Vincent Ferrer and St. Roch in the centre, St. Sebastian on the left, St. Dominic on the right, and in the lunette the Madonna of Mercy with St. Louis, a Dominican saint, St. Bernardino and St. Catherine, the palimpsest acquires a wholeness of vision through his confident mastery of perspective. Masters of the space within which they stand naturally on the gold ground, the figures have both a sculptural and a spiritual quality. In the three compartments, St. Sebastian stands transfixed gazing sorrowfully upwards while the other saints motion benignly and reassuringly towards the devotees. The Madonna of Mercy in the lunette is represented according to the ancient iconographic model but, like the saints around her, is given a human dimension thanks to the realistic use of «di sotto in su» (from below to above) perspective.

PIER MARIA PENNACCHI (1464-1514/15), *Death of the Virgin.* Oil on wood (1,34×1,69) – c. 1510.

Pier Maria Pennacchi is one of the most representative amongst Veneto artists of the late 15th century cultural climate. His artistic background was the figurative school of Treviso of the second half of the 15th century, where the influence of Antonello and Bellini as well as of Bramante and the northern artists was strongly felt. The connection between Pennacchi and Lorenzo Lotto, at work in Treviso in the first decade of the 16th century, is evident in the late work «Death of the Virgin». One also notes the influence of Giorgione in the use of colour.

ALVISE VIVARINI (c. 1446-1503/5), *«Sacra Conversazione»*. Tempera on wood (1,75×1,96) – 1480.

The heavy plasticity of Bartolomeo Vivarini and Andrea Da Murano was soon surpassed by the more balanced and harmonious three-dimensional quality of the works of Antonello da Messina. His St. Cassiano altar-piece of 1476, fragments of which are now in the Kunsthistorisches Museum in Vienna was studied and admired by a whole generation of painters. One of the first to be inspired by it was Alvise Vivarini, son of Antonio and follower of his uncle Bartolomeo, who soon went on to become a major exponent of Antonello's theories of crystalline form and colour. His major work coming from the first and much-admired studio of Messina is the «Sacra Conversazione» dated 1480, originally in the church of St. Francis in Treviso. The painting is composed with geometrical symmetry: the two groups of saints, Louis of Toulouse, Anthony of Padua and Anne on the left and Bernardino and Francesco Gioacchino on the right, face inwards towards the enthroned Virgin. In their gestures immobilized by the cold light which comes from the top left-hand corner, the three-dimensional figures appear to form a kind of architecture the centre of which is the throne, a construction of cylinders and parallelopipeds, behind which the curtain falls heavily excluding from sight all natural elements apart from two small fragments of a cold, clouded sky. Shadows appear to cut into the floor, confirmation of the geometrical relationship between space and figures, while the clear line delineates areas of pure enamel-like colour. This theory of formal abstraction was to become during the last few years of the 15th century still more monumental, in contrast to the ideas of colourization and sublime naturalness represented by Giovanni Bellini.

CARLO CRIVELLI (active 1457-1493), *St. Jerome and St. Augustine*. Tempera on wood (1,87×0,72) – c. 1490.

Carlo Crivelli was another of the young artists involved in the new developments taking place in Padua around the middle of the 15th century. But in his version of Renaissance naturalism, even more so than in that of Cosmè Tura, we can still see the influence of the Mediaeval traditions. Forced to leave Venice soon after 1467, Crivelli carried on his solitary activity in the Marches, developing an art rich in figurative detail and luminous in the clarity of form and colour. He was influenced by the wealth of culture which flourished at the court of Ferrara with the presence there of Piero della Francesca and Rogier van der Weyden. In his later works his sensitive approach to the intellectual search for technical perfection achieved, by means of a purity of line and colour, a refined and moving elegance. Evidence of this can be seen in the work «St. Jerome and St. Augustine», part of a triptych painted shortly after 1490 for the cathedral at Camerino. The intensity with which the two saints are portrayed against the gold ground, the linear vitality and the vibrant use of colour are impressive, as is the portrait of the lion with its metallic mane, its head raised in a roar, its claws gripping the marble.

ROOM 24

(The Albergo della Scuola)

The School's most valuable works were kept in the «Sala dell'Albergo». The «Sala» of the school of S. Maria della Carità still has the original decoration. The carved ceiling, altered in 1443/44 has rich gold and polychrome decoration around the central figures of the Holy

Father and the four Evangelists. The great triptych of 1446 by Antonio Vivarini and Giovanni d'Alemagna and Titian's «Presentation of the Virgin in the Temple» (1538) adorn the walls. Of the many gold and silver objects which the School possessed, only a reliquary remains here. It was given to the School by Cardinal Bessarion on August 29th 1463, the day of his admittance to the fraternity of the Carità, while he was trying as papal legate in Venice to persuade the Venetian Republic to take part in the crusade of Pope Pius II.

ANTONIO VIVARINI (c. 1415-1476/84) and **GIOVANNI D'ALEMAGNA** (active 1441-1450). *Triptych.* Tempera on canvas (3,39×2 central canvas; 3,39×1,38 side canvases) – 1446.

In this grandiose triptych Antonio Vivarini, helped by his brother-in-law Giovanni d'Alemagna, achieved a highpoint of balance between the International Gothic tradition now in decline, and the rising Renaissance (cf. p. 17). A natural light lends tenderness to the holy figures. The Virgin, however, sits rigid like a Byzantine empress on a Gothic throne, surrounded by Masolinoesque angels who are holding the poles of the high canopy almost as if it were a game. The saints Gregory and Jerome on the left and Ambrose and Augustine on the right, stand immobile in their heavy ecclesiastical garments shining with gold and colour. The holy scene appears constrained by the marble walls with their Gothic fretwork, set in a perspective as improbable as it is ostentatious. The sumptuous static scene is a final dazzling reminder of a fairy-tale world.

TIZIANO VECELLIO (TITIAN) (c. 1488-1576), *Presentation of the Virgin in the temple.* Oil on canvas (3,35×7,75) – 1538.

The young Titian studied in the mosaic workshop of Sebastiano Zuccato and then with Gentile and Giovanni Bellini. Inspired by the revolutionary painting of Giorgione, he developed his own artistic language from the latter's naturalism. Conversant with the ideas of Dürer, Raphael and Michelangelo by the end of the first decade of the 16th century, he renounced the contemplative world of Giorgione for the exuberant vitality of High Renaissance painting. His compositions seem to open out, the colours are infused with sensuousness and we witness the triumph of human passion and feeling, of Man who is no longer an enchanted figure but a very real presence. Titian's chromatic classicism reaches maturity in the third decade of the century. Later, influenced by Mannerist developments in Tuscany and Rome, he moves towards a monumental grandeur which at times shows the strain of «Classicist» tendencies. The «Presentation of

the Virgin in the temple» belongs to the beginning of this period; it was painted between 1534 and 1538 for the Sala dell'Albergo of the School of S. Maria della Carità. The painting which occupies the whole of the entrance wall seems to be a 16th century version of the narrative works of Vittore Carpaccio. The painting is composed with a scenographic figural rhythm; on the right at the top of the stairs the priest and his assistants await the tiny figure of Mary who appears even smaller in her halo of holy light against the ponderous architectural background. On the left stands the throng of onlookers, most of them outlined against the mountainous background, traditionally supposed to the that of the Marmarole in Cadore. The grandeur of the composition may appear studied and even academic but the painting of the elements which compose it is remarkable for the brilliant richness of the colour and interplay of tone. And amongst the host of individual portraits, each one drawn with a clear and immediate objectivity, we note in particular the four men dressed in togas. In their portrayal, full of monumental solemnity and individual energy, they are typical examples of Titian's value as portraitist of life in the 16th century. His objective observations are very different from the highly individual psychological investigations of Lorenzo Lotto (cf. p. 41).

INDEX of Artists

(Numbers in brackets refer to the respective rooms)